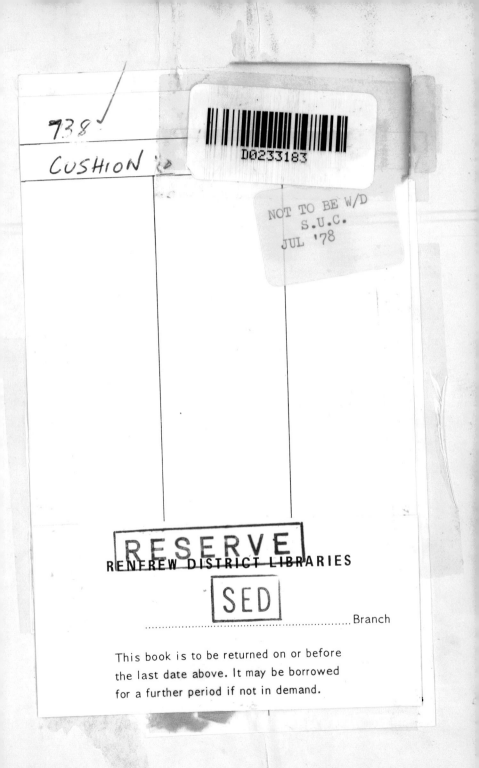

738

CUSHION

D0233183

RESERVE

RENFREW DISTRICT LIBRARIES

SED

.... Branch

This book is to be returned on or before
the last date above. It may be borrowed
for a further period if not in demand.

COLLECTORS GUIDEBOOKS

Animals in Pottery and Porcelain

I. HORSE, CHINESE, T'ANG DYNASTY (p. 11)

John P. Cushion

ANIMALS
IN POTTERY AND PORCELAIN

CORY, ADAMS & MACKAY

to Debbie and Cleo

© 1966 John P. Cushion
FIRST PUBLISHED BY CORY, ADAMS & MACKAY LTD
37 MUSEUM STREET, LONDON WC1
THE TEXT IS SET IN 'MONOTYPE' EHRHARDT
PRINTED AND MADE IN ENGLAND BY
W. &. J. MACKAY & CO LTD CHATHAM

Contents

List of Illustrations

7b Pair of cats, hard-paste porcelain modelled by J. J. Kaendler at Meissen (Dresden) about 1740, marked with crossed swords in blue. Ht. 7 in. *Antique Porcelain Co.*

8 A vulture, hard-paste porcelain, modelled by J. J. Kaendler at Meissen (Dresden) in 1734. Marked with the Crown and Cypher of Augustus Rex. Dated October 2nd, 1734. Ht. 23 in. *Antique Porcelain Co.*

9 A Bolognese hound of hard-paste porcelain, from a model by J. G. Kirchner. Meissen (Dresden), about 1733. Ht. 15¼ in. *The Metropolitan Museum of Art, New York*

10 and 11 Figures of Meissen hard-paste porcelain, painted with enamel decoration, known as the 'Monkey-Band'. Modelled by J. J. Kaendler about 1750, marked with crossed swords in underglaze-blue. Ht.'s 4¾ to 6¾ in.
Trumpet player, Drummer also playing the pipe, Kettle-drummer, Singer, Rattle player, Singer, Hurdy-gurdy player, Bagpipe player, Violinist, Pianist and Conductor
Flute player, French Horn player, Recorder, Singer, Bassoon player, Singer, 'Cello player and Guitar player. *Photograph by courtesy of Christie's*

12 Horse and groom, hard-paste porcelain painted in enamel colours, with French ormolu mounts. Modelled by J. J. Kaendler about 1750, at Meissen. Marked with the crossed-swords in blue. Ht. 11¾ in. *Formerly Rene Fribourg Collection*

13 Pelican of hard-paste porcelain, modelled by J. J. Kaendler at Meissen in 1732. Ht. 31 in. *Photograph by courtesy of Sotheby & Co.*

14 Honey-pot in the form of a bear, hard-paste porcelain. Modelled at Nymphenburg by Auliczek about 1765, mark of a hexagram in underglaze-blue. Ht. 9 in. *George Savage & Associates Limited*

15 Horse, hard-paste porcelain painted in enamel colours. Modelled by J. G. Becker at Höchst about 1770. Mark, a six-spoked wheel in red. Ht. 6 in. *Antique Porcelain Co.*

16a Pair of Lions of tin-glazed earthenware, made at Luneville about 1775. L. 17½ in. *Antique Porcelain Co.*

16b Boar of tin-glazed earthenware painted in enamel colours. Made by Paul Hannong at Strasburg about 1755. L. 8⅞ in. *Victoria & Albert Museum*

17a Dog, said to be a model of Madame Pompadour's own pet, soft-paste porcelain made at Vincennes about 1750. Ht. 7 in. *Antique Porcelain Co.*

17b Pastille-burner in the form of a hare, soft-paste porcelain decorated in enamel colours. Saint Cloud about 1750. Ht. 10½ in. *Victoria & Albert Museum*

18a Little Hawk Owl of soft-paste porcelain, made at Chelsea about 1752, marked with an applied anchor picked out in red. The engraving is Pl. 62 of George Edwards *Natural History of Uncommon Birds* (London 1743-7). Ht. 6¾ in. *Victoria & Albert Museum*

18b Goats of soft-paste porcelain painted in enamel colours, made at Chelsea about 1752, mark an applied anchor picked out in red. L. 6½ in. *Sotheby & Co.*

19a Tureen in the form of a rabbit, soft-paste porcelain decorated in enamel colours. Made at Chelsea about 1755, marked with an anchor in red. L. 14¼ in. *Victoria & Albert Museum*

19b Fox and Crane of soft-paste porcelain. Chelsea (Girl-in-a-Swing Factory) about 1751. Ht. 5½ in. *Museum of Fine Art, Boston, Mass.*

20a Boar of soft-paste porcelain, made at Derby about 1750-5. L. 5¼ in. *Victoria & Albert Museum*

20b Boar, a Roman marble copy of a lost Hellenistic original, now in the Uffizi, Florence. *Reproduced by courtesy of the Mansell Collection*

21a Lion, soft-paste porcelain made at Bow about 1750–5. L. 11½ in. *Dudley Delavigne Collection*

21b Lion, Roman marble from the Loggia dei Lanzi, Florence. *Reproduced by courtesy of the Mansell Collection*

22a Leopard with boy, soft-paste porcelain decorated in enamel colours. Made at Derby about 1758–60. Ht. 5½ in. *Leslie Slot Collection*

22b Hare of hard-paste porcelain painted in enamel colours. Made at Plymouth about 1770. Ht. 6¼ in. *Victoria & Albert Museum*

23a Equestrian figure of the Duke of Brunswick, soft-paste porcelain painted in enamel colours. Made at Longton Hall about 1760. Ht. 8½ in. *British Museum*

23b Hen and Cock, soft-paste porcelain decorated in enamel colours. Made at Bow about 1760. Ht. 4 in. *Victoria & Albert Museum*

24a Kingfisher, soft-paste porcelain. Made at Worcester about 1770. Ht. 5¼ in. *Rous Lench Collection*

24b Heron of soft-paste porcelain. Made at Longton Hall 1749–53. Ht. 4¼ in. *Rous Lench Collection*

24c Dog of soft-paste porcelain, modelled from a terracotta of Hogarth's pet 'Trump'. English about 1750. L. 11¼ in. *Rous Lench Collection*

25a Pug of salt-glazed stoneware, stained with manganese. Made in Staffordshire about 1745. Ht. 2 in. *Rous Lench Collection*

25b Mugs in the form of bears of salt-glazed stoneware. English, probably made in Staffordshire about 1750. Ht. 2⅞–3⅝ in. *Colonial Williamsburg Collection, Va.*

26a Tiger, 'Whieldon-ware' of 1750–5, made in Staffordshire. L. 7¾ in. *Rous Lench Collection*

26b Bird of 'Whieldon-ware', made in Staffordshire about 1750–5. Ht. 7½ in. *Rous Lench Collection*

26c Owl of Staffordshire 'slipware', about 1750. Ht. 12 in. *Rous Lench Collection*

27a Teapot in the form of an elephant with monkey and snake, earthenware decorated with coloured glazes. Made in Staffordshire about 1770 by Ralph Wood. L. 11 in. *Joan and Kenneth Chorley Collection, U.S.A.*

27b Two stags and a hind, earthenware decorated with coloured glazes. Made in Staffordshire about 1770–5 by Ralph Wood. Ht. 4⅛–8 11/16 in. *Colonial Williamsburg, Va.*

28a Horse of cream-coloured earthenware, decorated with blue, orange and black enamels. Probably made at Hunslet about 1835 from Leeds Pottery moulds. Ht. 16 in. *Leeds City Art Gallery*

28b Camel and dromedary, earthenware painted in enamel colours. Made in Staffordshire about 1830. Ht. 6¼ in. *By courtesy of Charles Mundy, Esq.*

29a Bull-baiting group, earthenware decorated in enamel colours. Probably by Obadiah Sherratt of Staffordshire about 1825. L. 11⅞ in. *Victoria & Albert Museum*

29b Three drinking-vessels in the form of pigs, red earthenware with lead-glaze. Made in Sussex during the early nineteenth century. L. 8⅛–15⅝ in. *Colonial Williamsburg, Va.*

30 Giraffe, Staffordshire earthenware decorated in enamel colours, about 1830–5. Ht. 13 in. *Dr. S. J. Howard Collection*

31 Owl, salt-glazed stoneware made in England (Southall) in 1899. Marked 'R. W. Martin & Bros., London & Southall, 3–1899'. Ht. 10½ in. *Victoria & Albert Museum*

32 Robin of hard-paste porcelain decorated in matt enamel colours. Made by Edward Marshall Boehm in 1964 at Trenton, N.J., U.S.A. Ht. 13 in. *By courtesy of E. M. Boehm, Esq.*

Introduction

MAN TODAY still shows a common habit with his early ancestors. When he is given a piece of soft clay or other such plastic material his immediate reaction is to form it into a shape—a simple ball rolled between the palms, a cube squared between the thumbs, or even a figure, sometimes in human form, but more often that of a familiar or fictitious animal. As soon as early man became aware of the properties of clay for making his primitive cooking-pots or bricks he as quickly realized the ornamental possibilities offered by this medium. From the times of Ancient Egypt, when bricks were merely strengthened with straw and dried in the sun, and throughout the ages, the various pottery materials in current use have been used for ceramic sculpture.

A wealth of material is encountered first in early China; fine vigorous animals made for tomb furnishing, monsters to ward off evil spirits and also simple farmyard pieces, probably made as playthings for the potter's children. With the introduction of glazes and the use of coloured slips, such figures became more pleasant to the touch and the eye, and there followed the large naturalistic camels and horses of the T'ang dynasty. When true or hard-paste porcelain was introduced its tight-fitting glaze left clear the fine modelling of the artist, who quickly saw the possibilities of this new glazed material for imitating the more precious hard-stones of jade and nephrite.

Porcelain wares had to be imported to Europe from the Far East until Augustus the Strong, Elector of Saxony and King of Poland, started his porcelain factory at Meissen. Augustus was responsible for the manufacture of more animals and birds than any other man, making unending demands upon the skill of the factory modellers. J. J. Kaendler, the most prolific of all porcelain modellers, worked to fulfil the King's lust for large figures of animals and birds to furnish his newly acquired *Japanische Palais*. When Augustus died in 1733 it already housed 439 models of animals and birds, from sixteen different moulds. The records go on to tell that during 1744, 35,798 pieces were produced from a variety of moulds. Thus it is not difficult to understand why constant reference has to be made to Meissen as the source of so many models.

The models of the soft-paste porcelain factories of France and England were often based on Meissen originals. At one time they were probably regarded as second-best, but now collectors have learned to appreciate fully the imitation porcelains with their subdued colours taken up by the glassy glaze, and their sensuous charm. It is to such wares that W. B. Honey undoubtedly referred when he suggested that, to be seen at their best, porcelain figures should not be larger than about seven inches, so that they could be easily handled and appreciated as a semi-precious ware.

From the early eighteenth century onwards the potters of Staffordshire found time to make figures of animals and birds in addition to the mass of useful wares. Astbury, Whieldon, and the Wood family have all given their names to types of figures undoubtedly made also by many other lesser-known potters. Later, in the nineteenth century, came the wares of Walton, Sherratt, Salt, and countless other Staffordshire figuremakers, and in Victorian times a mass of flat-back chimney-piece ornaments were cheaply produced for sale at markets and fairs.

It is the purpose of this book to acquaint collectors briefly with the materials, techniques, factories, and modellers concerned with the production of animals and birds made in pottery or porcelain, from the earliest times to the present. It will also perhaps inspire those who are not yet collectors, but lovers of animals, to begin to seek out such figures, however humble, and start collecting.

ACKNOWLEDGEMENTS

SINCE STARTING to collect material for this book I have met with only kindness and constructive help from everyone I have approached for either advice or photographs. Individual collectors, antique dealers, and museum personnel, both in England and America, have all made my task an easy and enjoyable one.

I would like to thank the following for their willing co-operation: Joan and Kenneth Chorley, Dudley Delavigne, Dr S. J. Howard, Leslie Slot, and the Rous Lench Collection.

The Antique Porcelain Co. Ltd, Asprey & Co. Ltd, Edward Marshall Boehm Inc, Charles Mundy, George Savage & Associates Ltd, Tilley & Co. (Antiques) Ltd, Christie, Manson & Woods Ltd, Sotheby & Co., the Mansell Collection and the Worcester Royal Porcelain Co. Ltd.

The authorities of the Ashmolean Museum, Museum of Fine Art, Boston, Mass., British Museum, Dept. of Collections, Colonial Williamsburg Incorporated, Virginia, Leeds City Art Gallery, Metropolitan Museum of Art, New York, and the Victoria and Albert Museum.

Materials and Techniques

EARTHENWARE, STONEWARE, and porcelain, both true or soft-paste, all require the essential ingredient of clay. The amount of vitreous material contained within clay varies, and kiln temperatures are adjusted accordingly, so producing materials with different finishes.

The most common example of earthenware is the simple red-earthenware flower-pot. Clay of this type was used in the early days to make vessels which were hardened by being laid merely in the heat of the sun, but they could, of course, only be used to contain dry materials or for storage. Earthenware clays vary widely in composition and appearance according to their locality. They are found in a variety of colours, the Staffordshire slipwares, for example, ranging from brownish-red to a creamy-white. They contain very little vitreous material, and consequently even after firing at temperatures of between 1,000° and 1,200°C they are porous. Often the term used for earthenware clay is 'terracotta' (Italian—'burned earth'). In order to make this type of pottery more useful, the body is usually covered with a glasslike coating of glaze, and this process not only makes the piece impervious to liquids, but also enhances the colour. If the glaze is an unsuitable match for the body, a minute crackling of the surface develops, called crazing, which allows liquids to penetrate and so stain the body.

The earliest glazes used in Ancient Egypt and the Near East were of the nature of soda-glass (alkaline siliceous glazes), with the addition of copper. Such glazes imparted a rich transparent turquoise finish to these early wares. The glaze more commonly used on earthenware by the Chinese and European potters was lead-glaze, consisting of sand or silica fused with the aid of natural sulphide, or an oxide of lead. As an alternative to lead, potash, often obtained from the lees of wine, was sometimes used. Pottery of the Chinese Han dynasty shows an early use of lead-glaze. The unfired clay was dipped into a lead-glaze mixture which when fired combined with the silica in the clay to form a transparent honey-coloured glaze. If the clay used was rich in iron, the glaze was stained to a yellow or brown, or if a green glaze was desired, as on so many of the Han

3

wares, then copper was used as a colouring agent. Blue was obtained likewise by the use of cobalt, purple from manganese, and black from a mixture of manganese and iron.

The colouring of glazes to add variety and to give scope of decoration to an otherwise dull clay was used to advantage by many earthenware potters, such as Bernard Palissy of France, Thomas Whieldon and Ralph Wood of Staffordshire and the tile-makers of Germany and Spain.

Lead-glaze is again seen on Near Eastern wares from the ninth century onwards, but now made white and opaque with the addition of calcined tin-oxide. The glaze was decorated first in the same high-temperature colours derived from metallic oxides, as described above, but from the middle of the eighteenth century the faïence potters of France fired the glaze first, and then, as on porcelain, added decoration in enamel colours which were fused to the surface of the glaze in a 'muffle-kiln' at a temperature between 700° and 800°C.

Some of the animals and birds illustrated and discussed will be of stoneware, a material commonly found in the form of marmalade pots, old-type ginger-beer bottles, or underground drainage pipes. Stoneware differs from earthenware in that the clay from which it is made contains sufficient natural 'fluxes' to enable it when fired at a temperature of between 1,200° and 1,250°C to vitrify, become a mass, and so be impervious to liquids. Some of the stonewares made in Germany during the fifteenth century were left without any further treatment, but most unglazed stoneware is unpleasant material either to handle or drink from. Fine red stonewares made from clays rich in iron are exceptions. *Yi-hsing* wares, exported from China during the sixteenth century, the red stonewares of Holland and Germany, and the wares of the Elers brothers of Fulham and Staffordshire, all have a very fine-grained, smooth, hard finish.

When a finer surface was required on stoneware it usually took the form of 'salt-glaze'. Salt, or sodium chloride, was thrown into the kiln at its peak temperature, and the sodium combined with the silicates in the clay to form a thin hard film with a fine 'orange-peel' surface. Here again the colour could be varied by the application of coloured oxides to the body of the wares before glazing. Enamel decoration could be fused to the glaze in a low-temperature kiln in the same way as on tin-glazed wares or porcelain.

The Chinese were not satisfied for long with the limited range of wares that could be made from earthenware and stoneware. It is thought that before the beginning of the Han dynasty (206 B.C.) they were aware of the value of china-clay (*kaolin*) and were making high-fired stonewares with a feldspathic glaze. Throughout the first eight centuries A.D. stonewares of a porcellanous nature were being made, but it was in the ninth century, during the T'ang period, that wares of true porcelain, both white and translucent, were produced in China. Such pieces were excavated on the site of the Abbasid capital on the Tigris, Samarra, a city that had been abandoned by A.D. 883.

Two essential clays are necessary for the manufacture of true porcelain, two ingredients aptly described by the Chinese as the skeleton and the flesh of porcelain. The first ingredient is china-clay, still known today as *kaolin*, a word adopted from the Chinese meaning 'high-ridge', after the area where it was apparently first found. China-clay is formed by the natural decay of feldspar or granite rocks. The second ingredient is china-stone or *petuntse* from the Chinese *pai-tun-tzu*, meaning little white blocks, the form in which the clay was sent to the potter after processing. China-stone comes from the same feldspathic rock, but it is in a less decayed state and far more fusible. It bonds together the particles of the white china-clay. When the two clays are fired to a temperature of about 1,300°C they form true hard-paste porcelain.

The powdered china-stone, with the addition of lime, potash, sand, or quartz, makes the feldspathic glaze required for true porcelain. The glaze can be applied to the wares before biscuiting, enabling fine porcelain, sometimes decorated with underglaze blue, to be completed in only one firing stage.

This method of manufacturing hard-paste porcelain remained a secret of the Chinese up to the time of the establishment of the German factory at Meissen. By the middle of the eighteenth century many other European factories had also learnt of the materials and the firing technique, but it was 1768 before the English factory of William Cookworthy was established at Plymouth, using both china-clay and china-stone from Cornwall. This material eventually resulted in the type of ware introduced in 1794 by Josiah Spode. It became known as bone-china and was made from 25 per cent. china-clay, 25 per cent. china-stone, and 50 per cent. of calcined animal bone or bone-ash. This body, with its creamy texture and extreme translucency, is softer than hard-paste, but more durable. Bone-china remains the standard body of most English translucent wares today.

The potters who were unable to gain knowledge of the ingredients of true porcelain or who did not know where they could be obtained, as was sometimes the case, were forced to produce a ware that imitated the finer material. The first and most famous of these soft-pastes was made at Florence in about 1575, under the patronage of Francesco Maria de' Medici, Grand Duke of Tuscany. A pleasing ware was made by firing together white clays with a glassy frit, and it was decorated in underglaze blue, the method so often used by the Chinese on their wares made especially for export. The factory at Florence was short-lived and only about sixty examples of 'Medici' porcelain are known to exist.

John Dwight of Fulham was obviously endeavouring to manufacture a true porcelain in 1671, when he took out patents for making 'a transparent earthenware, commonly known by the names of porcelaine or china', but all he succeeded in making was a very fine salt-glazed stoneware, which is sometimes actually so thin that a faint translucency can be observed.

In France, experiments made at Rouen and Saint Cloud from about 1673 resulted in a fine creamy soft-paste porcelain, much like the porcelain later produced at the early English factories. There is no documentary evidence, however, to suggest that the English porcelain manufacturers came by their recipes by any means other than their own experiments. Most soft-paste porcelain has as a basis the ingredients of glass made into a glass 'frit' and then ground to a powder. This forms the substitute for china-stone and provides the translucency, while a white clay, with lime as a purifier, takes the place of china-clay and gives the necessary opaque quality. The varying proportions of such ingredients used by the different factories help us today by means of chemical analysis to determine the factory at which an example was made. This was an important factor when investigations were being made regarding the products of two Chelsea factories.

The earliest Chinese wares were made by 'coiling'. In this method vessels were built up with ropes of clay and the ridged walls were then beaten smooth. To make the process easier, a 'slow-wheel' was introduced, enabling the potter to slowly rotate the growing form rather than walk around it himself. Further developments resulted in the fast-moving wheel used today. These methods are, of course, only applicable for circular forms; the production of irregular figures requires a different technique.

The major difference between most pottery figures and sculptured terracottas is that pottery figures have generally been made from moulds cast from an original model, and can thus be reproduced in large numbers as required, whereas a sculptured terracotta is the original free-hand work of the modeller and can only be reproduced by the same laborious process.

6

II. MONKEY BY J. J. KAENDLER, MEISSEN (p. 21)

The modellers of the original figures worked in many mediums. Clay, wax, or even wood was used to create the master model, and the modeller had to be conversant with the technical requirements, for he could easily make it difficult for those who had to work from the original figure. Shrinkage had to be taken into account and also the tendency for unsupported limbs and similar parts to sag when the firing temperature reached its peak. The mould-maker had to cut the master model into pieces, free from undercuts which would lock the cast into the mould, and easily removable from the mould. Porcelain paste has little plasticity and a modeller would find it difficult to model the figure initially from such material, even if it were an economic proposition. The negative shapes offered by the moulds are essential in order to support the figure until it is dry enough to retain its shape.

Early Chinese figures were made by pressing the sheets of clay into simple fired-clay moulds, often consisting of only two pieces. A back and front of a simple tomb figure would thus only require joining down the side-seams with 'slip' (watered-down clay). This process of joining up the various pieces cast from the moulds has to be carried out while the clay is in a moist state, known as 'cheese-hard', otherwise the application of wet slip to a dry clay would cause uneven expansion with the resultant cracking.

The major continental porcelain factories used this 'press-moulded' technique, but assembled the two or three pieces of the mould with the pressed clay still in position, and then swilled a wet paste inside to weld the pieces together. These moulds could be used for up to about twenty-five figures; if further models were required, new moulds could be made from the original model or a plaster replica. Where it is possible to see inside a figure through the base it is possible to determine whether this process was used. Such figures are generally heavy and have walls of varying thickness scored by tool-marks or with impressions of the potter's fingers. Among the English factories using this process of casting were Bow, Plymouth, Bristol, and Worcester.

The alternative method to 'press-moulding' is 'slip-casting'. Here the various sections of the mould are assembled completing a 'negative' of the shape required, and this hollow shape is then filled with slip. (The clay of either earthenware or porcelain, when watered down to a creamy consistency is termed slip.) The water in the slip immediately starts to penetrate the plaster wall of the mould and in so doing builds up a deposit of clay on the inside of the mould. When the workman knows from experience that the required thickness of clay has been reached the remainder of the slip still within the assembled mould is poured off, and in a short while the mould is opened and the completed cast carefully removed. The various parts of the figure made in this fashion are then assembled to a standard pattern by the 'repairer', using slip once more as an adhesive.

This method of slip-casting was in use from at least 1740. It was by such means that the potters of Staffordshire made their finely moulded salt-glazed stonewares such as teapots in the form of houses or camels. This method of casting quickly wore out the moulds, and the salt-glaze potters found it an advantage to make a fired stoneware master block, from which countless casts could be taken. The Chelsea, Derby, and Longton Hall factories all used the 'slip-casting' method to produce their figures.

The fact that pottery and porcelain shrinks when fired makes it necessary to have a small hole from which the gases trapped within the hollow shape can escape. The shape or position of these holes is sometimes a guide to the factory; early Derby figures, for example, have a 'funnel-shaped' hole, as though it had been reamed out to counter-sink a screw. The square holes on the back of many Bow figures were intended for the location of metal bocage fittings that were sometimes added to support a candle-holder together with porcelain flowers.

There are a large variety of ways in which pottery and porcelain can be decorated. These are best dealt with in the following chapters devoted to the various wares which have been used during the last two thousand years to make figures of animals and birds.

China, Japan, and the Near East

CHINA

IT IS GENERALLY accepted among ceramic collectors that the finest pottery and porcelain ever made is of Chinese origin. Dating from the end of the Stone Age (approx. 2500–1500 B.C.) is a class of fine, hard, reddish earthenware jars, made by the technique of 'coiling' with ropes of clay. These wares were apparently used as mortuary urns and vary considerably in size. Figures of a comparable material or period do not appear to have been made, or have not been identified.

The earliest Chinese dynasty of which we have knowledge is that of the Shang-Yin period, dating from about 1600 to 1030 B.C. From this date the Chinese potters made many unglazed wares in imitation of the fine contemporary bronzes. It was not until some time in the succeeding Chou dynasty (c. 1030–256 B.C.) that methods for the deliberate glazing of pottery were discovered.

We owe the survival of many figures to the long-established practice of placing pottery models in tombs. Excavations of graves dating from the late Chou period at Hsi-Hsien, Honan, have brought to light a wealth of interesting material. Such wares were seemingly made as a cheap form of more precious metals and they were termed *Ming-ch'i*, meaning 'that which is for the usage of the dead'. This practice replaced the earlier barbaric custom of human sacrifice and the actual internment of the things that the deceased was likely to require for his comfort in the afterlife. During the Sung dynasty (A.D. 960–1279) the pottery tomb furniture gave way to similar articles in wood, and these, of course, have not survived like pottery. Today the custom is continued by the burning of paper images.

It is from the period of the Han dynasty (206 B.C.–A.D. 220) that tomb figures and others are found in large numbers. Typical of such pieces is the model illustrated on Plate 3B showing a sheep pen, complete with sheep and mounted shepherd. Here we have the use of a lead-glaze made green with the addition of copper; a new beauty is given to many such wares by the colourful surface iridescence, caused by the partial decay of the glassy glaze during its long burial. A large variety of animal forms are found among such figures even at this early date; nearly all the animals of the farmyard with their appropriate dwellings, dogs and kennels, pigs and sties, and even fishponds, were made in miniature to meet the needs of the deceased.

Great importance was attached to the *Ming-ch'i* and the correct placing of the individual pieces within the tomb. In the case of a military personage the retinue comprised what amounted to a funeral procession; cavalry, standard-bearer, musicians, drummers, and various dignitaries and attendants numbering about seventy-five pieces would be placed around the coffin. During the T'ang dynasty regulations were enforced as to the number and size of the *Ming-ch'i*. It was standardized according to the rank of the deceased, the numbers ranging from ninety pieces for a 'Very Important Person' to fifteen for a commoner. It has been suggested that a person visited the model-maker and chose the figures that he preferred to have with him at a later date.

It cannot be said that these early figures had any tendency towards delicacy. On the contrary, they are usually exceedingly lumpy, and give the feeling of clay sculpture in its early stages of making; this is well illustrated in the vigorous figure of the rhinoceros (Plate 2a). In this instance the animal is partially covered with an olive-green glaze. There must also be some doubt as to whether an animal of this species was intended for tomb furnishing.

Horses were, of course, a necessity for both the deceased and his attendants, and so there are many early forms of this animal in a variety of postures. One interesting form is a horse made up in separate sections; the head and the neck are made to dowel into the robust body, but on the underside of the body, where the legs would normally be, there are only holes. The legs would probably have been carved from wood and a real hair tail have been added. Such horses are often decorated in red and white unfired pigment.

The period between the Han and T'ang dynasties is known as the Six Dynasties, a time that has been referred to as the Dark Ages of China, when the country was divided under several rulers and subject to many invasions from Central Asia, and consequently the progress of many forms of art suffered. The production of sculpture and bronzes continued almost alone, and indicates increased following of Buddhism; the few pottery wares attributed to this period can sometimes be dated by their similarity to such examples, but it is generally the rare dating of excavated tombs which gives an authentic year to the contents.

The horse shown in such an unusual pose (Plate 1) is a fine example of a tomb figure and it is considered to date some time during the Six Dynasties. During this period there was a movement towards finer detail and realism; the modeller no longer relied solely on a good form, and it is noticeable that even simple figures of ducks and other birds were incised with lines to simulate feathers and other details.

Of special importance during the Six Dynasties was the introduction of a fine high-fired stoneware or proto-porcelain. Made in Chekiang from some time in the third century, these Yüeh wares contained clay of a fusible nature that was rich in feldspar, and this material was eventually to develop to form the first white, translucent hard-paste porcelain in the world. It is rather surprising to find it being used to make nicely modelled pieces, merely for burial, of sheep in pens and pigs in sties, as seen in the Ashmolean Museum, Oxford.

The guardian lion (Plate 3a) illustrates yet another form of animal modelling dating some time between the Han and T'ang dynasties. The purpose of this ferocious lion was to ward off any evil spirits from the deceased, and it would have been positioned near the mouth of the tomb. The lion is, of course, sacred to Buddhism and from the time of the Six Dynasties he is increasingly used in many forms of art. One of the many essentials for the tomb equipment was a wagon, generally drawn by a pair of oxen; Plate 2b illustrates a very complete assembly of such a wagon, dating about sixth to seventh century. There are very few genuine examples of this particular model in existence, because of its complicated and fragile form.

With the accession of the T'ang dynasty (A.D. 618–906) the *Ming-ch'i* became even larger and more prolific; the figures took on a new naturalism and rhythm of movement and their beauty was enhanced with coloured glazes. Tomb figures were now made of a soft pinkish earthenware with a coating of white slip; many were covered with a lead-glaze and attempts were made to pick out the details of the harness and saddle in high-temperature colours (coloured frontispiece). Alongside such fine horses are comparable camels, often shown laden with articles of the trade which they normally carried on the overland caravan routes between China and Islamic Iran and Mesopotamia. The best of these animals appear to have an individuality of their own, and one of the finest examples of such a camel is in the collection of the British Museum. It stands about thirty-three inches high, and is an authenticated model from the grave of

Chancellor Liu T'ing-hsün, who died in A.D. 728. Caution must be exercised when such figures appear very unusual, for many horses and camels have been re-formed from broken and dull pieces and made up into more interesting postures by skilled 'repairers'. An early suggestion by W. B. Honey that the 'fighting stallions' from the Eumorfopoulos Collection had been reconstructed in this manner has since been proved correct.

During the late T'ang dynasty the secret of the manufacture of true porcelain was discovered and in the period of the Five Dynasties (A.D. 907–959), linking the T'ang and Sung, the improvement of wares in this new material continued and a great deal of porcelain was exported as far as the Middle East and Japan. The Sung dynasty (A.D. 960–1279) is of particular importance for the production of high-fired stoneware and porcelain. The practice of burying large quantities of cheap earthenware in the tombs largely discontinued, but a certain amount of lead-glazed wares which are hard to precisely date were undoubtedly still made in the early Sung period.

The 'scratching' lion (Plate 4a) is a fine beast showing lively modelling in the new porcelain of early Sung. This piece was possibly the lid of an incense-burner and its bluish-grey glaze is one of several classes of the so-called celadon glazes. Apart from a late class of figures made at Tz'u Chou from a stoneware covered in cream-coloured slip and decorated with red and green enamels, almost the entire Sung dynasty was devoted to the manufacture of superior vases and dishes illustrating many varieties of beautiful glazes often made in imitation of bronzes or jades.

The great Ming dynasty (A.D. 1368–1644) has often been referred to as the Renaissance period of China. Ming means 'Bright' and this epithet can certainly be applied with truth to the ceramics of these three centuries, for after the comparatively sombre Sung wares the colourful Ming pottery looks almost bizarre. The city of Ching-tê Chên took on a new importance as the ceramic centre of China when the Emperor Hung Wu decided to establish there in 1369 an Imperial kiln for the production of porcelain, most of which was decorated in underglaze blue.

From the start of the Ming dynasty it became the practice to write on the base of wares the mark of the reigning Emperor. If the porcelain potters of China had continued to be honest when applying such marks, the identification of porcelain from the fourteenth century until 1916 would be very simple, although probably very dull. The marks very soon became quite untrustworthy, particularly during the reign of the Emperor K'ang

Hsi, when porcelain was generally marked with the names of earlier Ming
Emperors such as Hsüan Tê, Ch'êng Hua, and Chia Ching, during whose
reigns some very fine porcelains were actually made.

During the Ming dynasty, as in the Sung, very few figures were produced in either earthenware, stoneware or porcelain which preserved a
continuity in spirit with earlier T'ang examples. Ridge-tiles are an interesting exception. These tiles were used on the corners of the roofs of
buildings and were initially intended to fend off evil demons; they took
the form of horsemen, dragons, fighting-men and many other fantastic
shapes. Their quality varied, but they were nearly all glazed in the bright
high-temperature colours.

From the time of the Ch'ing dynasty Emperor, K'ang Hsi (A.D. 1662–
1722), there was a noticeable influence throughout China of Western
fashions and styles in all the popular arts. In 1680 the Emperor set up an
Imperial kiln in the city of Peking itself, but this idea did not prove
practicable and by 1682 an Imperial factory had been re-established at
Ching-tê Chên. It is difficult to visualize at that early date a city where,
according to Perè d'Entrecolles, over a million people were working on the
production of porcelain, involving the use of more than three thousand
kilns. Porcelain now took on an almost monotonous look of perfection,
and the wares are of such refinement that it is difficult to appreciate that
they have been made by hand from a plastic clay.

The majority of figures made in the K'ang Hsi period were of the
famille verte; this *wu ts'ai*, or five-coloured painting, was in two shades of
green, iron-red, yellow, and aubergine. These coloured glazes were in
most cases applied directly on to the 'biscuit' porcelain, in preference to
fusing enamel colours on to a previously glazed piece. This technique was
used to make numerous small figures, such as lions or Dogs of Fo, horses,
elephants, and parrots, the latter group having been the subject of many
recent forgeries.

In the past much confusion has arisen over the various symbols and
motives used in Chinese art, and probably no two mythological animals
have been more subject to misnomers than the Kylin and the Dog of Fo
(Plates 4b and 5b).

The Kylin was considered in China in much the same way as the Unicorn in Europe. It was a completely legendary animal, half male (Ch'i)
and half female (Lin), hence Ch'i-lin or Kylin. This beast was naturally
very rarely sighted by mere mortals, but if one should have had that good
fortune it was considered an omen of longevity, grandeur, and felicity,

and foretold the advent of a virtuous ruler. The Kylin is one of the four great mythical animals of China, the others being the Dragon, the Phoenix, and the Tortoise. The outward appearance of this harmless creature belies its good intent; it has the body of a deer covered with a scaly hide, the head of a dragon coupled with a goatlike beard, the bushy tail of a lion, cloven hoofs, and a single fleshy-tipped horn, entirely unsuitable for use in combat. The Kylin was thought to have a life span of a thousand years, and during that period never once did it tread upon another living creature or destroy plant-growth with its footsteps; it fed only on vegetation and drank only from clean waters. Some Chinese writers suggest that this creature was seen at the time of the birth of Confucius, but it ceased to show itself because man had so degenerated. Others even go so far as to say that the mother of Confucius became pregnant by stepping into the footsteps of a Kylin on her way to the hills to worship.

Reproductions of this creature have been made throughout the centuries from a variety of materials and in many sizes, but they are hard to find in pottery and porcelain. Dogs of Fo or Guardian Lions, however, are encountered far more frequently. These lions are generally found in pairs, as illustrated, the male at play with a brocaded ball, while the female is more fully occupied with one or more cubs. The lions were usually made to serve a useful purpose and have small cylinders attached which were intended to hold joss sticks. The true lion is not, of course, indigenous to China, and it was not depicted in primitive art, but gifts of such animals were most probably received by Emperors of the T'ang dynasty (A.D. 618–906). The Chinese interpretation of this animal is usually of a ferocious and frightening guardian rather than an attacker and it was particularly associated with Buddhism as a defender of law and a protector of sacred buildings or tombs. Dogs of Fo were made in great quantities during the reign of the Emperor K'ang Hsi from A.D. 1662 to 1722 and later.

Some time during the first quarter of the eighteenth century a new opaque rose-pink colour was introduced to China for the decoration of porcelain which was intended primarily for export. This is the colour 'borrowed' from Europe, which gave the name to a new class of porcelain known as *famille rose*. During the reigns of the Emperors Yung Chêng (1723–35) and Ch'ien Lung (1736–95) a great many porcelain birds were made which often included this rose-pink enamel in the palette. The birds were generally of an exotic type: cocks, hawks, cranes, pheasants, and the phoenix were all depicted, usually standing on a rocky mound. Great experience is necessary to attribute these figures correctly to a period, for the production of them has continued in China until today, and in addition many copies have been made in Europe. A close examination of the quality of the material, the glaze and the painting and a comparison with documentary specimens is absolutely essential.

From the seventeenth century many birds and animals have been made in the beautiful white porcelain from the kilns of Tê-hua in the southern province of Fukien. This material has a colour range varying from a warm white to a pale grey and its glaze is fine and well fitting, giving the appearance of opaque glass.

JAPAN

The amusing lion illustrated in Plate 5a is seemingly resentful that he is the lone example of Japanese porcelain in this book. Porcelain is unlikely to have been made in Japan until the sixteenth century, when kilns were established in the neighbourhood of Arita, in the Hizen province. The early wares were mostly decorated in a poor quality underglaze blue, but by 1700 the Dutch traders were shipping to Europe large quantities of the so-called Imari wares, decorated in a confusing and fussy manner with chrysanthemums and scrollwork in blue, red and gilding. A more pleasing decoration is the so-called Kakiemon style, said to have been introduced by a potter of that name about 1650. This figure of a lion is decorated in the palette of Kakiemon with distinctive shades of green, blue, turquoise, and yellow.

NEAR EAST

The potters of the Near East had no access to ready supplies of either china-clay or china-stone, the two clays essential to the making of true porcelain, but from the twelfth century this deficiency was made good by the introduction of a translucent white composition which had much in common with some of the earlier soft-paste porcelains of Europe. The cat illustrated in Plate 6b is made of this material and dates from some time in the first half of the seventeenth century; it was made at Meshed, where, according to the writings of Chevalier Chardin in about 1670, some of the best Persian pottery was produced. It is no ordinary cat, for apart from being a 'Persian', it forms the water-container of a 'hubble-bubble' tobacco-pipe. A metal tube from the pan of burning tobacco ran down through the vessel into the water, and when the smoker inhaled through a tube from above the water-level the smoke was drawn through the water. Wares of the same material as that of the cat are also quite commonly found in the forms of sitting birds, to be used as 'bath-rasps' to soften the skin on the soles of the feet.

The Persian style of painting in underglaze blue was so similar to that of the Chinese that evidence has recently come to light that a great deal of Persian ware was shipped to Europe by the Dutch East Indies Company during the third quarter of the seventeenth century, when because of unrest in China it was difficult to obtain porcelain for export.

The jug in the form of a horse (Plate 6a) is by comparison relatively modern, but such examples of Turkish peasant-ware are encountered surprisingly often in this country. Horses and camels were made in this style at Chanak Kalé on the Dardanelles during the nineteenth century. They are of a reddish earthenware body and decorated with various coloured slips and glazes, and are easily distinguished by their 'cotton-reel' legs. Another common type of vessel from this same area is the tall, bulbous, long-necked jug terminating in an animal mouthpiece, usually decorated with crudely applied flower designs under a green or brown glaze.

German Porcelain

THE MATERIALS required and the technique of manufacturing true, or hard-paste, porcelain was until 1710 the closely guarded secret of the Far East. We are today so familiar with ceramic materials in varying forms, that it is difficult to appreciate with what admiration the fine porcelains of the Ming period (A.D. 1368–1644) were regarded by both the Chinese themselves and Europeans. The ships of the East India Companies were concerned primarily with tea and silks, but in addition enormous quantities of porcelain were shipped, often conveniently as ballast, being, of course, impervious to any damage by sea-water. By the second decade of the seventeenth century ships of the Dutch East India Company were docking with as many as 200,000 pieces of Chinese porcelain aboard, mostly the fine blue-and-white made during the reign of the Emperor Wan Li (A.D. 1573–1619). Under the reign of the Ch'ing Emperor K'ang Hsi (A.D. 1662–1722) the trade in porcelain between China and Europe grew to even more fantastic proportions.

The potters of Europe had up to this time only been able to imitate such wares by using the familiar technique of adding a lead-glaze, made white and opaque with the addition of tin-oxide, to a lightly fired earthenware body, and decorating it with the metallic oxide of cobalt. This blue colour when painted on the unfired glaze was able to withstand the comparatively high kiln temperature necessary to fire the glaze and it is referred to as a high-temperature colour. The Dutch were particularly skilled at making slavish copies of Chinese porcelain in this manner. It was produced mostly at the small town of Delft during the second half of the seventeenth century, the craftsman even going to the length of adding a further clear lead-glaze, known as *kwaart*, in an endeavour to complete the illusion.

Attempts to imitate the Chinese porcelain wares had resulted in varying forms of soft-pastes being introduced first at Florence, in Italy, in the second half of the sixteenth century, and again about a hundred years later at both Rouen and Saint-Cloud in France, but it was Germany that eventually, and quite independently, rediscovered the closely guarded secret of the Chinese. Soon after his accession in 1694 the Elector of Saxony, Augustus II 'the Strong', King of Poland, directed Ehrenfried von Tschirnhausen, an experienced chemist and physicist, to undertake a survey of the mineral wealth of Saxony. This research was intended to be mainly concerned with semi-precious stones and the manufacture of glass comparable to that of Bohemia, but it would appear that Tschirnhausen himself was particularly interested in discovering the necessary raw materials for the production of Chinese-type or hard-paste porcelain, partly to help stem the flood of currency leaving his country for the purchase of immense amounts of the sought-after Chinese table-wares. The alchemist Johann Friedrich Böttger is a name more widely known, and at times he is rather unjustly given the entire credit for the rediscovery in Saxony of the means of making porcelain, but from 1704 he was working with Tschirnhausen. By July 1708 they had together succeeded in manufacturing a form of unglazed porcelain, using a white-burning clay from Colditz, near Zwickau, together with a calcareous flux in the form of alabaster. The Colditz clays were very shortly replaced by clay of a superior quality discovered on the estate of Johann Schnorr von Carolsfeld at Aue in Vogtland, whilst the alabaster was later replaced by the correct ingredient of feldspar. The Royal Saxon Porcelain Manufacture was finally established, with the issuing of a patent, on 23 January 1710, and within two months it was housed in the Albrechtsburg fortress at Meissen, twelve miles outside the city of Dresden.

It is opportune here to explain that when referring to this first hard-paste porcelain factory of Europe the term Meissen is preferable to that of Dresden, for during the nineteenth century many smaller establishments were set up in the city of Dresden. These were generally only for the decorating of porcelain which was supplied in the white from various minor German factories. The decoration was usually in the mid-eighteenth-century styles and marks were adopted with the obvious intention of confusing the purchaser with the wares of the original factory.

Augustus the Strong had by this time acquired a superb collection of Far Eastern wares. With the object of providing a suitable building to house both these pieces and the porcelain from his own factory he purchased, in 1710, from his Field-Marshal Count von Flemming, a palace which was renamed the Japanisches Palais.

The early years of the factory were devoted to the manufacture of table-wares, lavish services and fine garnitures of vases, many of which were exported to foreign courts. It was 1727 before a sculptor, Johann Gottlob Kirchner, was engaged to take charge of figure modelling, and after only a year Kirchner was dismissed for being 'flighty and frivolous'. He was replaced by a well-known ivory-carver, Johann Cristoph Ludwig von Lücke, who also proved unadaptable at producing models suitable for reproduction in this new plastic material of hard-paste porcelain. In 1730 Kirchner was re-engaged and shortly afterwards made the *Modell-meister*, and in the next year, 1731, came the appointment by the King of another sculptor, the now famous Johann Joachim Kaendler (b. 1706). The two former sculptors worked together until 1733, when Kirchner was finally dismissed.

The production requested by Augustus of imposing figures and vases of Meissen porcelain to furnish his Japanese Palace was commenced during Kirchner's first period of employment. It was in this period some of the finest large animals ever made appear. The precise dating of such early figures is difficult, as is also their positive attribution to a particular modeller. The so-called Bolognese Hound (Plate 9) from the Metropolitan Museum of Art, New York, is generally regarded to be an early work of J. G. Kirchner. This is a rare example of such a large piece bearing additional enamel decoration. These masses of porcelain were difficult to fire without excessive shrinkage causing fire-cracks, and to submit them to a second firing in a muffle-kiln to fuse the enamels to the glaze was a very hazardous procedure; consequently the majority of such animals, most of which are still housed at Dresden, were either left in the white or were decorated with unfired lacquer colours, most of which have now worn off. Another similar model of slightly later date and considered to be the undoubted work of Kaendler, was featured in the sale of the Rene Fribourg Collection (Part II) at the auction rooms of Sotheby & Co, London, on 15 October 1963; this model was mounted on a fine pierced and chased ormolu mount of the Louis XV period. In general the animals and birds thought to have been modelled by Kirchner have a fairy-tale character, whilst his rival Kaendler appears to have made much greater use of the fine gallery of stuffed animals in the Natural History Collection in the Zwinger, the outstanding example of German baroque built by Matthäus Daniel Pöppelmann between 1711 and 1722 for the main purpose of pageantry and theatrical performances. In addition Augustus's love of hunting called for a zoo of live animals. Lions, bears, leopards, lynxes, foxes, apes, and wolves were kept in captivity in the Jägerhof at Dresden-Neustadt, and an aviary of exotic and ornamental birds, available for modelling from life was housed at the Moritzburg Castle, between Dresden and Meissen. The aim appears to have been to make these early animals as large as life. Typical of such pieces are the pair of goats; the male figure in the Victoria and Albert Museum was sold from the Dresden Collection in 1919 and is certainly life-size (height 22 in, length 26 in). Its companion figure of the female with kids is shown in the Ashmolean Museum, Oxford. Both these pieces are badly defaced with fire-cracks.

From the beginning Kaendler was superior to his partner in the realism of his modelling. He seemed to have had an immediate grasp of porcelain as a material, and a feeling for its qualities, using the reflective advantages of the glaze to emphasize the more intricate modelling. The Vulture (Plate 8) is typical of his work; this example is a rare dated specimen, twenty-three inches high. Incised on the inside of the hollow tree-trunk is the crown and cipher of Augustus III as King of Poland and Frederick Augustus II as Elector of Saxony, together with the date 2 October 1734. Similar large pieces were made even of elephants, although not full size in this case, four feet high being about the maximum. A pair of such animals is to be seen at Longleat in Wiltshire, the home of the Marquess of Bath. Lions, apes, dogs, polar bears, rhinoceroses and birds such as the vulture, necessitated the building of a special kiln. An extremely rare model of a pelican is shown on Plate 13. This bird is now considered to have been modelled by Kaendler in 1732; it is a vigorous figure, thirty-one inches high and twenty-nine inches long. The unavoidable fire-cracks are again very apparent on this model. The use of a higher proportion of china-clay than normal in these figures resulted in the material being rather greyer than expected with the fine porcelain of Meissen. In 1900 only two such models remained in the Dresden Collection of the ten *Loeffelgans* which appear to have been there originally.

Augustus the Strong died in 1733 and was succeeded by his heir, Frederick Augustus II, whose main preference in art was for painting rather than porcelain. As a result the direction of the factory was left in the hands of Count Heinrich von Brühl, who in turn had complete confidence in the abilities of his modeller Kaendler. In addition to the elaborate services showing the high relief modelling made under the direction of Kaendler, many figures of animals and birds continued to be made at the factory, sometimes showing the hand of his assistant, Johann Friedrich Eberlein, who came to Meissen in 1735. The models of this period are of more modest proportions and in addition to many hunting scenes depicting dogs hunting bison, stags, wolves, bears, or boars,

Kaendler modelled very large numbers of birds of superb quality. Parrots appear to have been an especial favourite of this modeller, and between 1731 and 1745 he is credited with modelling fifteen different varieties of this bird. In Part I of the Fribourg sale on 25 June 1963 some very fine models of swans were sold, ranging from five to eleven inches high; these undoubtedly were originally made to feature in what may well rank as the most ambitious porcelain service ever assembled, the famous 'Swan Service' made for Count Brühl soon after his appointment.

Doves, ducks, drakes, woodpeckers, cockatoos, jays, crows, sparrow-hawks, and peacocks were all in turn modelled by Kaendler around the seventeen-forties, and these are the figures which have been copied to such a large extent in the second half of the nineteenth century. The original figures were either unmarked or bore the small underglaze-blue device of crossed swords, the mark adopted from the Electoral Arms of Saxony in 1724 and still in use by the factory today. The later reproductions invariably have an underglaze-blue mark sufficiently similar to confuse the unwary, and are the work of minor Thuringian factories of Germany or often by the firm of Edmé Samson et Cie, of Paris. To the beginner these hard-paste reproductions are not too readily detected. Close study of originals in public collections is required and particular attention to the palette, for the pastel shades of green and pink derived from chrome are certainly indicative of nineteenth-century work.

Monkeys seem to have held a fascination for both Kirchner and Kaendler and they were made over a long period in many sizes. The Ape illustrated (Colour Plate II) is attributed to Kirchner and is of exceptional size ($17\frac{1}{2}$ in); the fine candle-holders and mount of Louis XV ormolu were probably added in France. Similar, though smaller figures of monkeys are recorded with both ormolu mounts and bocage added, the latter being decorated with soft-paste porcelain flowers made at the French factory of Vincennes (later to become the Royal factory of Sèvres). Lazare Duvaux, the dealer in such wares to the French Court, records such a sale to Mme la Princesse de Royan in 1751.

Probably the best known and also the most copied of Meissen monkeys are the so-called Monkey-Band or *Affenkapelle*, some of which are shown for reference on Plates 10 and 11. This particular group was sold at Christie's, the London auctioneers, on 4 March 1963. Although the monkeys are said to have been modelled in 1747, their manufacture appears to spread over a long period, but as can be clearly seen they have the typical rococo bases of this middle period. The London factory of

Chelsea was copying such models in its soft-paste porcelain during the red-anchor period of that factory (1752–6); they further feature in the Chelsea Sale Catalogue of 1756 under Lot 57, described as 'A set of five monkies in different attitudes playing on music'. The oft-repeated story that the band was made originally in ridicule of Count Brühl's orchestra is, of course, a story without any apparent foundation. The most common continental copies of these monkeys were made in the nineteenth century by a factory using a mark in underglaze blue suggesting a pair of open scissors, a mark so far unattributed to any specific factory.

Kaendler's talents were unlimited and in his modelling of horses he again appears to be unsurpassed for realism (Plate 12). The inspiration for most of these fine horses is considered to be the renowned Lipizzaner horses from the Spanish School of Equitation in Vienna. In contrast to the rococo bases of the Monkey-Band, the simple flower-strewn mound base is clearly of a slightly earlier date. The fact that these were reproduced by the Staffordshire factory of Longton Hall about 1755 suggests a date of at least five years earlier, in addition to which the fine Louis XV ormolu bears *poinzons* of the crowned 'C', a mark used only until 1749.

Among the smaller animals modelled by Kaendler were many varieties of dogs. The later Bolognese Hound already mentioned was a firm favourite, as was also the *Möpser*, a pug dog of a breed especially popular at that period. This model is one made at the later English factory of Longton Hall. Kaendler even featured the mouselike Jerboa (Plates 7a and b).

The creator of these most sought-after Meissen figures died on 18 May 1775. His models reflected the baroque taste right to the end of his forty-five years with the factory, and they were to remain the models most copied by numerous other factories for many years.

HÖCHST

The first four years of the factory established at Höchst on the Main in 1746 were devoted to the making of faience. The man responsible was yet another who had received his schooling at Meissen, Adam Friedrich von Löwenfinck. In the early years some very fine large animals including parrots were made, together with numerous tureens in the form of pheasants, turkey-cocks, boar's heads, and ducks. Many of these finer pieces are today attributed to the modeller J. G. Becker, who had studied under the Meissen modeller Kaendler, and who worked at Höchst from 1746 until 1755. Later earthenware reproductions of some of these early models were made from about 1830 by Daniel Ernst Müller of Damm, using the original moulds.

In 1750 came the arrival at Höchst from Vienna of Johann Benckgraff who with the aid of J. J. Ringler produced a fine quality hard-paste porcelain, rather opaque, with an exceptionally milky-white glaze. The mark adopted was the six-spoked wheel from the arms of the Elector of Mayence; at first the mark was applied to the glaze in red enamel or gold, but from about 1762 the more customary method used by the German factories of underglaze blue was adopted. Between 1765 and 1774, the Electoral Hat or Crown was added to the wheel mark. The rare figure of a horse (Plate 15) is the only known example of this model. It can be dated precisely, as it was given as a prize at a porcelain lottery held in Höchst on 4 September 1770, when it was described as a Rearing Horse. The base with its rococo-scrollwork surround is very indicative of this factory at this period; later bases took the form of a natural grassy mound.

By about 1760 the call for figures in German porcelain, both in human and animal form, seems to have been very limited, and was restricted mainly to useful wares such as tureens made in the form of birds. With the competition of the now flourishing soft-paste porcelain from the Royal factory of Sèvres, all the German porcelain factories were concentrating on producing well-decorated table-wares in the restless but spirited style of *Louis Seize*. As the following Neo-Classical movement gained ground the material of porcelain was soon recognized as being an unsuitable medium to suggest the works of early antiquity, although the porcelain left in the 'biscuit' stage and devoid of all additional decoration was for a time popular for its mimicry of the beauty of Classical marble.

NYMPHENBURG

By the middle of the eighteenth century the closely guarded secret of the manufacture of true porcelain, or 'arcanum' as it was called, was no longer known in Europe by Meissen alone. The Vienna factory of Du Paquier was making true porcelain by 1719, to be closely followed by the short-lived Venetian factory of the brothers Vezzi in 1720. Renegade workmen, having learnt the secrets of the necessary clays and also how to construct the kilns capable of reaching the high temperatures, a factor of equal importance, were often prepared to desert and sell their knowledge to the highest bidder. Many factories owe their successful establishment to Joseph Jacob Ringler, who deserted from Vienna in 1747; one such factory is that of Nymphenburg in Bavaria, where we find Ringler working from 1753 until 1757. Experiments had been started here with the support of the Elector Maximilian III Joseph, but nothing except faience appears to have been manufactured until the arrival of Ringler.

The fame of Nymphenburg is undoubtedly due to the outstanding ability of one of their modellers, Franz Anton Bustelli, who came to the factory in 1754 and was the Director of Modelling until his death in 1763, at the early age of forty. Doubt has recently been cast as to the correctness of this last date by Dr Carl Gräpler of Munich, for the name of Bustelli was a fairly common one in those parts. The most widely known of Bustelli's models, which he carved from lime-wood, are those depicting characters from the Italian Comedy. His treatment of bases deserves special mention, for he used the wavelike motion of the rococo theme, to take the place of the all too obvious pedestal or tree-trunk which had been necessary as a support to the more delicate figures during the firing stages of their production.

It is to Bustelli's successor, Dominkus Auliczek (b. 1734), that we look for the realistic animal groups of this factory. As if with the deliberate intention of producing figures and groups with an entirely different feeling to those of his predecessor, these groups border almost on the sadistic. Auliczek is known to have made twenty-five such groups, most of which have been left in the white, usually clearly marked with the impressed shield from the arms of Bavaria, or with the so-called 'hexagram mark' (a six-pointed star shape, composed of two reversed triangles). The honey-pot illustrated in Plate 14 is typical of the realism of the modelling of Auliczek and is a rare study. Prior to his arrival at Nymphenburg, Auliczek studied sculpture in Vienna, Paris, London, and Rome, where in addition he took a three-year course in anatomy. In 1762 he was in Munich, having been let down by a would-be patron who had promised him an important post in the Court, and thus he was still available when Bustelli's post of *Modellmeister* became vacant. He was persuaded by Von Haimhausen, the Director and Administrator of the Nymphenburg factory, to fill the position. His more usual groups depicting the full cruelties involved with the Court pastime of hunting are well known; he appeared to revel in the careful modelling of the blood-thirsty injuries, which if they had been painted in colour would have been distinctly sickening.

FÜRSTENBERG

The porcelain factory of Fürstenberg in Brunswick has had a long history,

III. SQUIRREL, RED-ANCHOR CHELSEA (p. 36)

having been founded by Duke Carl I in 1747 and being still in production today. In *German Porcelain and Faience* (London, 1962), Siegfried Ducret relates how the Court enthusiasm was so great at the establishment of the concern that the Duchess Philippine Charlotte threw out all her old porcelain under the impression that the material could be melted down and used again.

The mark of the cursive 'F', used in slightly varying forms over such a long period, is difficult to date accurately. The earlier wares show many faults in the shape of black specks in the paste. The outstanding modeller of this factory was without doubt Simon Feilner, who was employed from 1754 until 1768, when he was discharged for being lazy and insubordinate. Apart from the fine Italian Comedy figures modelled by Feilner, he is recorded in the factory archives as producing equestrian figures and animals. Leuenberger, another modeller of about 1755, is given the credit for having modelled a fine group in the Brunswick Museum of a lion attacking a horse. In 1775 Johann Christoph Rombrich and Anton Carl Luplau were actively engaged in reproducing versions of some of Feilner's earlier models, together with copies and original versions of the famous Monkey-Band, previously discussed under Meissen.

LUDWIGSBURG

This factory of Wurtemberg was producing porcelain from 1758 until 1824, and again the name of the arcanist J. J. Ringler is recorded, now as the first Director of the porcelain factory of Duke Charles Eugene, claimed by him to be 'necessary to the splendour and dignity' of his realm. The modeller most worthy of note in this instance is Jean-Jacob Louis, whose original work has been identified by an incised 'L'. This 'chief repairer', who was engaged from 1762 until his death in 1772, had first developed his modelling skill at Tournai, and many finely modelled birds, especially parrots and animal groups, are ascribed to his hand. The wares of the Ludwigsberg factory were generally marked during the life of Charles Eugene (d. 1793) with two interlaced 'C's under a ducal coronet.

FRANKENTHAL

The severe restrictions forced upon Paul Hannong whilst working at Strasburg by the monopolies granted to Vincennes (later Sèvres) made it necessary for him to transfer his production across the river to Frankenthal, where he enlisted the support of the Elector Palatine, Carl Theodor.

After the death of Paul Hannong in 1760 the factory was run by his son, Joseph-Adam Hannong, until 1762, when because of mounting debts the concern was purchased by the Elector. The paste of Frankenthal was of a fine quality from about 1755 until 1775, when the hard creamy-white paste was covered with a thin white opaque glaze which readily absorbed the enamel decoration. It did not obscure the fine modelling of artists such as J. W. Lanz, who worked at Frankenthal from 1755 until 1761. The early figures of Lanz show bases similar to Strasburg, in the form of a simple mound. Featuring in Hannong's 1760 price list are two fine figures of stags, one standing, the other leaping, about five inches in length and bearing the impressed mark of 'PH' for Paul Hannong.

French Porcelain

THE FRENCH were the second people in Europe to succeed in making a fine soft-paste porcelain in imitation of the Chinese true hard-paste wares. The early history of French porcelain is a little confused; the earliest would appear to have been that at Saint-Cloud, following a privilege granted in 1664 to Claude and François Révérend for the manufacture of porcelain but due to confusion as to the meaning of the word porcelain at that time their products are thought to have been only a type of faience.

According to Dr Martin Lister's book on his travels, written in 1698, there was a potter named Morin with a factory at Saint-Cloud who, after experimenting for many years, succeeded in about 1695 in making porcelain of such a high standard that Dr Lister wrote, 'I confess I could not distinguish betwixt the pots made there and the finest China ware I ever saw', but here either Dr Lister's appreciation was at fault or he was seeing a type of Saint-Cloud porcelain with which we today are still unacquainted.

The other Saint-Cloud factory of which we have more certain knowledge is that established by Pierre Chicanneau, who died in 1678. The following year Chicanneau's widow married Henri-Charles Trou, who secured for the factory the protection of the Duc d'Orléans, although it appears that Trou himself never possessed the secret of the manufacture of porcelain which they claimed to have perfected in 1693. Upon the death of his wife in 1722 a renewed patent was taken out by the son, Henri II. The factory remained in the family of Trou until 1766, when it went into liquidation.

There is still doubt as to the sure identification of porcelain made at Rouen following a patent granted in 1673 to Louis Poterat. In 1694, when Poterat applied for the renewal of a faience privilege, the question of his porcelain was taken up by the authorities and it seems that he had made a limited amount of this material entirely unaided in order that his workmen should not sell his secrets to rivals.

The early wares of Saint-Cloud and the few examples attributed to Rouen are all table-wares and vases, and it is the second quarter of the eighteenth century before Saint-Cloud produced some interesting animal forms. The soft-paste porcelain of Saint-Cloud is of a warm ivory tone, usually rather thickly potted in the baroque style, with a good glassy glaze with minute surface pitting. The larger pieces tend to develop fire-cracks and slight warping is often apparent. The fine pastille-burner in the form of a hare (Plate 17b) must date about 1750, when the factory was working under difficulties because of the Vincennes monopoly. During the second quarter of the eighteenth century some beautiful snuff-boxes were made in the form of sheep and other animals, and these can often be dated precisely by their fine silver or gilt mounts.

A further soft-paste porcelain factory was established in 1725 at Chantilly by the Prince de Condé; this concern carried on until about 1800 under a long succession of proprietors. The best porcelain was made in the first twenty-five years of the factory, and during this time tin-oxide was generally added to the glaze to give the appearance of hard Oriental porcelain in keeping with the 'Kakiemon' style of Japanese painting which was the most usual form of decoration at Chantilly during this period. Wares for the table again formed the major part of the production and animals only appear in the guise of finely potted bonbonnières or other 'toys'. The mark of Chantilly was a hunting-horn, first in red enamel, later in underglaze blue, and both these marks are frequently encountered on nineteenth-century reproductions.

The third most important early French soft-paste porcelain factory was Mennecy, established first in Paris by the Duc de Villeroy in 1734 and transferred to Mennecy in 1748. In 1773 it was again transferred, this time to Bourg-la-Reine, where it remained until 1806. It is likely that the last years saw only the production of cream-coloured earthenware, such as made universally popular by Josiah Wedgwood. The fine milky-white porcelain with a brilliant glaze was particularly hit by the stringent monopolies granted to Vincennes and Sèvres; the lack of gilding which they were not permitted to add to their graceful forms is especially missed. Figures were made at Mennecy, usually bearing the 'D.V.' mark (Duc de Villeroy), and especially charming are the groups of children, seemingly after Boucher, which have a strong likeness to Bow. The few animal groups that are recorded were usually based on Meissen or other German originals, such as a 'Monkey riding on a hound' and a squatting monkey, but otherwise it is again only in the form of snuff-boxes and similar articles that sheep, rabbits, etc, are once more seen.

The factory of Vincennes was first established in a disused Royal château near Paris. Gilles and Robert Dubois claimed to have learnt the secrets of porcelain manufacture during their employment at Chantilly and so a nobleman, Orry de Fulvy, financed their attempts with help from the King. They were unsuccessful up to 1741, when they were discharged, and the venture was continued with the help of yet another disloyal worker from Chantilly, François Gravant. In 1745 a good soft-paste porcelain was seemingly produced.

A company was now formed in the name of Charles Adam and the first of the privileges was granted, attempting to eliminate competition from other French manufacturers. The company was given the exclusive right for a period of twenty years to manufacture 'porcelain in the style of the Saxon (meaning Meissen), that is to say, painted and gilded with human figures'. In 1747 a further privilege prohibited the other manufacturers not only from making porcelain but also from hiring Vincennes workers. It is obvious that through their influential patronage the three factories previously discussed continued to operate in defiance of these orders, but their productions were undoubtedly controlled.

The many artists of the Court were directed to apply their skills to this new medium, including such people as the goldsmith, Duplessis, the enameller, Mathieu, and the chemist, Jean Hellot. The staff of the factory quickly grew, until in about 1750 over one hundred were employed. Orry de Fulvy died in 1751 and a further company under the name Eloi Brichard was formed, the King himself again subscribing a large sum. In 1753 further harsh restrictions even endeavoured to prevent the manufacture of faience if decorated in colour, and the Royal Cipher of the crossed L's was declared to be the accepted factory mark; date letters within the crossed L's (e.g. A=1753, B=1754, etc) were used from now, although the L's alone had been used for several years previously. A start was made in 1753 on a new building for the factory at Sèvres, between Paris and Versailles. This factory was eventually occupied in 1756; debts quickly accumulated and by 1760 the factory was entirely the concern of the King.

The fine soft-paste continued to be the only material made at the Royal factory until 1769, when deposits of china-clay and china-stone (*kaolin* and *petuntse*) were acquired at Saint-Yrieix, near Limoges. From 1772 the soft-pastes gradually gave way to the new porcelain, until in about 1800, when Alexandre Brongniart was appointed by Napoleon to take over the administration of Sèvres, the earlier material was abandoned as being too costly.

The unsurpassed table-wares made by this Royal factory are well known. The first early wares, under the influence of the renegade work-men, were in 'Japanese-Chantilly' style, with copies of decorations made popular by Meissen. In the second period, from 1753 to 1772, the simpler forms gradually gave way to large and often overdecorated vases of the type so well represented in the Jones Collection at the Victoria and Albert Museum, and the Wallace Collection at Hertford House. Vincennes and Sèvres porcelain can often be judged on the quality of its gilding alone. The knowledge of their process was originally purchased for a large sum from Frère Hippolyte, a Benedictine monk, and a particularly attractive use of this gilding was made by Mutel, who applied heavy gilt relief birds in silhouette to a clear porcelain reserve on a ground of underglaze blue (*gros bleu*).

Antoinette Poisson, or the Marquise de Pompadour, despite her humble parentage, was quick to acquire an appreciation of beautiful objects, and it was she who persuaded Louis XV to subsidize the factory. The dog illustrated in Plate 17a is a rare early figure of about 1750 and is reputed to be the Marquise de Pompadour's dog. The early figures of Vincennes were original models and it is difficult to identify the individual work of the various modellers named in the factory records. Other animals appear in the contemporary lists of productions, but are very rare; among such pieces is a fine figure of a water-spaniel of about 1755—the dog is nearly a foot in length and is covered with turquoise glaze on an enamelled base. The registers of the Sèvres sales also mention birds decorated in blue or 'lapis'.

In about 1753 it became fashionable at Sèvres to leave figures in the 'biscuit', that is unglazed, and this fashion continued during the next forty years. Some time prior to his appointment to the factory in 1757 the sculptor Etienne-Maurice Falconet had been modelling for the factory, but his work, much influenced by Boucher, was usually of nymphs or children and there appears no record of his having made any figures of animals or birds.

French Earthenwares

ALTHOUGH THE knowledge of the manufacture of hard-paste porcelain remained the closely guarded secret of the Chinese for around eight hundred years, the method of disguising cruder earthenware to look like porcelain was quick to spread across Europe from Mesopotamia. It came first from the hands of the potters of Islam during the ninth century to the southern shores of the Mediterranean. It was adopted in the fourteenth and fifteenth centuries in Spain during the occupation by the Moors at such centres as Valencia, Manises, Malaga, and Granada. These Hispano-Moresque wares with their fine painting in 'golden' metallic lustre illustrate some of the finest free brushwork of the pottery artist. Such wares were soon to be exported to Italy by way of the Balearic Island of Majorca, and so for the Italian tin-glazed wares we arrive at the term *maiolica*.

In Italy during the last quarter of the fifteenth century the city of Faenza was the most productive centre in the country of this new industry. Emigrant Italian potters were soon to introduce their methods to the Low Countries, France, and England. The wares were to be known later as *faïence* in France, *fayence* in Germany, while the popular name of *delft-ware*, used in England and Holland, was not adopted until the seventeenth century.

The early tin-glazed earthenwares of France, made at such centres as Rouen, Lyons, and Nevers, are hard to distinguish from the Italian wares which they closely imitated, and apart from the occasional figure of an ecclesiastical nature the entire output of faience at this period was of useful wares.

Until the middle of the eighteenth century faience and tin-glazed wares of other countries were decorated with colours derived from metallic oxides which were capable of standing the same high temperature (*grand feu*) that was necessary to fire the glaze, and thus the decorators were confined to a rather limited palette. Varying shades of green were obtained from copper, blue from cobalt, purple from manganese, yellow from antimony, and orange from iron. All these colours were painted on to the raw glaze before firing, a process requiring a sure hand, for mistakes could not be rectified, except by washing off the entire coating of powdered glaze and starting afresh.

The middle of the eighteenth century found the tin-glazed earthenware potters all over Europe in competition with the manufacturers of porcelain. The soft-paste porcelain of both England and France was enjoying great popularity and in addition Chinese porcelain was available through the various East India Companies in increasing quantities. It thus became necessary for faience to be decorated in a similar style to that of the more fashionable ware. The colours fired with the *petit feu* offered a new exciting range of reds, crimsons, pinks, and blues. These metallic colours were compounded with powdered glass and merely fused to the surface of the glaze, which had been previously fired, in a low-temperature muffle-kiln at a temperature ranging around 800°C.

During this phase animals and birds in naturalistic colours were made for the first time in France. The factory at Lunéville (Lorraine) dates from 1723 and continued throughout the nineteenth century. Lions such as those illustrated in Plate 16a appear to have been a speciality of this factory. These recumbent creatures are exceptionally large (length $17\frac{1}{2}$ in.) and were often set in doorways or used as garden ornaments; their production was continued during the next century by the later proprietors of the Lunéville potteries, Keller and Guérin.

The important factory of Strasburg has already been mentioned in connexion with Frankenthal porcelain. Its position so near the German border and the fact that wares exported to Germany were subject to a lower duty than those sold within France itself, resulted in the Strasburg factory, and others in the east of the country, catering mainly for German tastes, and imitating in their styles the porcelain of that country.

The Strasburg factory started in 1721 and remained in operation until 1780. During these sixty years the Hannong family produced wares of such importance that their styles still remain among the most reproduced of tin-glazed earthenwares. The founder of the concern was Charles-François Hannong, whose son Paul acted as manager from 1732 until 1739, when he became Director. The faience made in these early years was decorated in the limited range of high-temperature colours, with an occasional use of gilding.

From 1748 great improvements were made in the wares produced at Strasburg through the employment of skilled artists and modellers who had previously worked at the porcelain factory of Höchst. Through their technical knowledge Paul-Antoine Hannong became the first faience potter to use the full colour range of the *petit feu*. The fine figure of the boar (Plate 16b) is a rare model and much influenced by the porcelain figures then being made in Germany. Most of the animals made from earthenware were in the form of large tureens, and many fine examples are recorded, such as turkeys, pigeons, and boar's heads, There is one particularly celebrated tureen in the form of a large duck which deserves special mention, modelled by the German, J. W. Lanz—the bird is fourteen inches in length and is the only example known complete with a separate oval stand; this model was sold at Sotheby's on 15 October 1963 (Fribourg Collection, Part V). Among the smaller models in the German tradition made to serve as table decorations are sets of huntsmen, leaping stags, and orchestras.

The colour so often used in the palette of Strasburg that it is a pointer to the factory is the well-known deep crimson, known by the more romantic name of 'purple of Cassius', a colour derived from gold; this same colour was also used by the Chinese on their porcelain made especially for export, when, from about 1725, they were catering for the so-called 'foreign devils'.

When Paul Hannong died in 1760 he was still manufacturing hard-paste porcelain in Frankenthal; the venture was continued by his son Joseph, who was compelled to sell to Elector Palatine Carl Theodor in 1762. Joseph then returned to take charge of the Strasburg faience factory, but the factory never again reached the high standard set by his father and it failed in 1780. The much-copied monogram of 'PH' was used from 1739 to 1760, whilst from 1762 until the close the initials used were 'IH'.

The famous factories of southern France were at Moustiers, Saint Jean du Désert, and Marseilles, but these produced few figures of any type, preferring to concentrate on beautiful free decoration on good practical shapes. Pigeons in the form of tureens are rare, but examples are known and bear the fleur-de-lis mark of Honoré Savy. Savy was first a partner at the Veuve Perrin factory, but from 1764 he ran his own factory with great success.

English Porcelain

AS DRESDEN is to German porcelain, so Chelsea is to English, the names most commonly associated with the finest and earliest porcelains of their type in Europe. One vast difference is that while Meissen (Dresden) was producing true hard-paste porcelain as early in 1710, the London factory at Chelsea was throughout its life concerned only with the manufacture of an artificial soft-paste.

The history of the Chelsea factory is one of the easiest of porcelain undertakings to memorize, falling clearly into five clearly defined periods; the triangle period, the raised-anchor, red-anchor, and gold-anchor periods, and the final period from 1770 until 1784 when the factory was taken over by William Duesbury, the proprietor of the Derby factory, and which is referred to by collectors as the Chelsea-Derby period.

Very little porcelain produced at Chelsea was entirely original in either form or decoration, for it would have been difficult to invent a new acceptable style, able to find a ready market, that had not previously been made fashionable by the Meissen factory of Saxony or one of the early French factories. French influence was only to be expected, as Nicholas Sprimont, the founder of the Chelsea works, was himself born at Liège. He was by profession a silversmith, entered at Goldsmiths' Hall in 1742, and his manager, Charles Gouyn, was a French jeweller and china dealer who came to this country some time prior to 1745. Both these men must therefore have been well acquainted with the early soft-paste porcelain of such factories as Saint-Cloud, Chantilly and Mennecy.

In collecting circles the first period of Chelsea is now regarded as lasting from 1745 until 1749. It was the period of the first Sprimont-Gouyn partnership, and during this so-called 'triangle period' the mark most commonly used was a small triangle incised into the base of the object prior to the initial firing. The paste of this first period has great similarity to that of the late seventeenth-century factory of Saint-Cloud; it is milky white in colour and has a very glassy appearance, and apparently it did not lend itself easily to the manufacture of German-type figures. The well-known model of a teapot formed by a paunchy Chinaman with a parrot which serves as a spout is an amusing figure subject found in this early period.

A rare animal subject considered to be of this first period of Chelsea is a small figure of a greyhound, marked with the rare device of a crown intersected with a trident. This mark is in underglaze blue and it is difficult to suggest a reason why a factory which so seldom used this colour to decorate its wares should now choose it for a rare mark. The greyhound, measuring five inches in length, is so superior in modelling to any contemporary English figure that it was considered by Arthur Lane to have been cast direct from a bronze or ormolu original. This piece was undoubtedly made by the 'slip-cast' method of reproducing such models (as described under 'Techniques'); the key-workers of the Chelsea factory, who are said to have been recruited from the Staffordshire potteries, must have been well versed in this process, which had been used for making complicated shapes in the high-fired salt-glazed stoneware since at least 1740.

The second period of Chelsea dates from 1749 until 1752, when the mark adopted by Sprimont to identify a new improved paste was a small anchor standing out in relief on a small oval pad of clay, generally applied to figure subjects in a fairly conspicuous position. This 'raised-anchor' paste, which was to prove so superior to the original material, is less glassy in appearance. Recent research has proved that the glaze used on most wares of this period contained a small amount of tin-oxide, which accounts for the distinctly white opaque appearance.

Many figures derived from the earlier Meissen factory were produced in this period. Through his patron, Sir Everard Fawkner, Sprimont gained access to a large collection of Meissen porcelain belonging to Sir Charles Hanbury Williams, the British plenipotentiary in Dresden, and at that time stored at Holland House in London. The many human figures made after the German originals are outside the scope of this book, but of outstanding merit are the series of about twenty birds. They are original to Chelsea factory and were inspired by some engravings published in 1743.

The Natural History of Uncommon Birds was by George [Edwards, Library Keeper to the Royal College of Physicians. The volumes are now rare and were the result of twenty years of study and drawing of birds from nature. Edwards was particularly proud of the fact that he had 'for variety's sake, given them as many different turns and attitudes as I could invent': 'Great complaint hath been made, that a late writer on birds hath given his birds no variety of posture, but that they are direct profiles, standing in the same position, which sameness is disagreeable.' George Edwards was justifiably proud of his accomplishment; he even went to the length of receiving personal instruction in the art of engraving or etching on copperplates in order to maintain the high standard he desired. He presented a copy of his work, in four parts, to the Royal College of Physicians, as a standard work of reference by which the true colours of the birds could be verified.

As can be seen in Plate 18a, the Chelsea porcelain modellers made an excellent job of their reproductions within the limitations of the difficult material of soft-paste porcelain. They were not, however, of sufficient merit to please the original artist, for in Vol. I of his *Gleanings of Natural History* (1758) Edwards says: 'I have observed that several of our manufacturers that imitate China Ware, several print sellers, and printers of linen and cotton cloths, have filled the shops in London with images, pictures and prints, modelled, copied or drawn, and coloured after the figures in my *History of Birds*, most of which are sadly represented both as to shape and colouring . . . the world can form but a mean opinion of the work from which they are plundered, unless they examine the original itself.'

William Duesbury (b. 1725, d. 1786) is probably best known as the proprietor of the Derby factory from 1756 until his death, but of far greater interest to collectors are the many porcelains and stonewares of other factories which passed through his hands when he was working in London from 1751 to 1753 as an independent decorator. Although there seems to have been little shortage of skilled potters, many of whom came from Staffordshire, the same was not the case with decorators. Many of the figures that now appear to have been left in the white were undoubtedly at one time decorated in unfired colours which have since worn off. The notebooks of Duesbury from 1751 to 1753 tell of painting such wares for an average of half a crown, whereas his 'inhamild' decoration usually trebled the cost of unfired painting. The early group of goats (Plate 18b) is today generally accepted, without any positive proof, as being by the hand of this prolific decorator.

The fine, naturalistic Chelsea squirrel (Colour Plate III) is a rare model, unmarked, made about 1752, and once again inspired by the earlier Meissen modeller, Kaendler, who modelled a similar figure in 1732. The earlier model, an example of which was sold by Sotheby & Co. on 25 June

1963 (Fribourg Collection, Part I), is marred by the animal wearing a heavy black collar fastened to the base with a gilt chain; the base is decorated in the customary early Meissen style with applied foliage and flowers. The Chelsea figure illustrated seems a much happier squirrel, free from tethering, more liberally decorated, on a simple mound base, and representing Chelsea figures at their best. Although based on the German figure, the actual modelling is original work and slightly larger.

Many late reproductions when cast from moulds made from an original are quickly identified as reproductions, since they are smaller than the earlier figure by just the amount of shrinkage which would occur during the first firing in the 'biscuit' kiln; this is often the case with copies made by Samson of Paris during the second half of the nineteenth century. In this respect one must not overlook the fact that some factories such as Derby made some of their later figures, particularly their biscuit groups, in more than one size.

The Victoria and Albert Museum owes much to Lady Charlotte Schreiber, who in 1885 presented to what was then known as the South Kensington Museum a truly remarkable representative collection of English pottery and porcelain, nearly all of the eighteenth century. The *Journals of Lady Charlotte Schreiber* (ed. M. J. Guest, 1911) tell of her travels throughout Europe in search of rare examples for her collection. Lady Charlotte Elizabeth Bertie was born in 1812, daughter of Albemarle, 9th Earl of Lindsay. At the age of ten Charlotte, enduring an unhappy childhood because of a difficult stepfather, commenced to keep a diary which she maintained for sixty-nine years. In 1835 she married the wealthy iron manufacturer, John Joseph Guest, and despite his being twenty-seven years older than his wife the marriage was a great success, and when her husband died he had fathered a family of ten children. In addition to her love of the arts Lady Charlotte now also took over as managing director of the Welsh ironworks.

In 1855 Charlotte again married, this time to her elder son's tutor, Charles Schreiber. Ten years later Lady Charlotte Schreiber became obsessed with a passion for collecting and for the next fifteen years this amazing couple toured Europe in search of treasures. In addition to the collection of English ceramics which she gave to the nation in 1885 she collected European and Oriental porcelain and earthenware, playing-cards, fans, and furniture. In 1884 Lady Charlotte was again widowed, and she spent her remaining years cataloguing her collections and doing charitable works; her diaries ceased in 1891 through blindness and in

1895 Lady Charlotte Schreiber, the self-styled 'China Maniac', died.
The diaries of her travels tell of many bargains which this astute
collector found, such as the delightful tureen in the form of a life-sized
rabbit (Plate 19a), inspired by the love of naturalism at the banqueting-
table in Germany. The rabbit is marked with the small red anchor of the
1752–6 period of the Chelsea factory and was purchased in Rotterdam,
'where we obtained a magnificent large rabbit of old red-anchor Chelsea
at van Minden's, very cheap. Would only it had been perfect—still it is a
noble piece. He only asked £5 for it and took £4.' This same trip saw the
purchase of 'A Chelsea pug (tail replaced) 10/-'; 'At Block's only two
little Bow cats (13/4d)'.

A more common tureen is that in the form of a life-sized hen and chicks
on a large moulded platter, decorated with sunflowers and easily identified in the sale of wares from the Chelsea Porcelain Manufactory, held
for sixteen days in 1756, at the Great Room of Mr Ford in St James's,
Haymarket. The piece is listed as 'A most beautiful TUREEN in the shape
of a HEN and CHICKENS *as large as life* in a fine sunflower leaf dish'.
Similar tureens are listed in the shapes of a boar's head, swan, drake, and
partridges while other animals listed for the 'desart' (dessert) or table
decoration include cows, sheep, cow and calf, goats, ewes, Bantam cock
and hen, lambs, fox, dog, and '5 monkies in different attitudes playing on
musick'.

An interesting figure shown in Plate 24c is still the subject of much
discussion as to its manufacture. Meissen is generally looked to as the
origin of most English and French animal and bird subjects, and great
similarity is also often found between the wares of Vincennes, the early
Sèvres factory, and Chelsea of the raised-anchor period, but no prototypes
are likely to be found for this very important dog. This model is of the
favourite pet of William Hogarth, the artist. The animal enjoyed the name
of Trump, and was said by some of Hogarth's enemies to look much like
his master; this well-known dog appears in a self-portrait by Hogarth,
dated 1745, and now in the Tate Gallery, London. While appearing to
have been made at the Chelsea factory, a chemical analysis made of the
material showed a very strong content of silicate of magnesia or soapstone
(steatite), and this is a material generally expected only in the porcelains of
early Bristol, Worcester, some of the Liverpool factories, and Longton
Hall in its later years. The model is considered to have been made from a
model in terracotta by Louis François Roubiliac, the famous French
sculptor, who worked in England from 1731 and has often been said by

earlier writers to have been associated with the Chelsea porcelain factory
as a modeller. We know from records that Nicholas Sprimont was god-
father to Roubiliac's daughter Sophie in 1744, but there is no proof as yet
of any closer association with the factory, and the most obvious conclusion
would be that Hogarth permitted moulds to be taken of his terracotta,
which remained in the possession of Mrs Hogarth until her death in 1789.
Arthur Lane, in *English Porcelain Figures of the Eighteenth Century* (Faber
& Faber, 1961), even proposes Longton Hall as an acceptable suggestion
of the factory responsible. On the other hand, one has to appreciate that
all the major English porcelain factories of the mid-eighteenth century
were constantly experimenting and endeavouring to improve their pastes
by trying out recipes acquired from other factories through disloyal work-
men, and therefore to limit the results of the chemical findings to the
evidence produced by one extremely rare figure could be misleading.

The gold-anchor period of Chelsea is today considered to date from
about 1758, a few years later than previously accepted. Nicholas Sprimont
was suffering ill health during 1757, but despite this the output of the
factory appears to have continued, for in 1758 sufficient wares were
accumulated to warrant a fourteen-day sale in Dublin, Ireland, of Chelsea
porcelain, though this may, of course, have included wares produced in
previous years that had remained unsold in England. The change-over
from the red-anchor period to that of the gold anchor spread apparently
over quite a long period and did not necessarily indicate a particular new
phase in the life of the factory. The major change concerning these two
periods was in the material; the fine white glaze of the raised- and red-
anchor years was now replaced by a much glassier glaze, which was very
prone to crazing (minute crackling), especially when in thick pools, and
whenever the glaze tended to gather it took on a distinct greenish hue.
The paste also changed and liberal use was made of calcined bone-ash, a
material that had been used by the London factory of Bow from early years.

Porcelain fashions were now to be dictated by Sèvres. Meissen in
Saxony was in a state of war, the Seven Years War with Prussia having
started in 1756, and so the French factory faced little opposition from their
earlier rivals. The age of rococo had arrived and the simplicity of the
former figures was now replaced by rich coloured grounds with a tendency towards overdecoration in both colour and lavish gilding. Figures
were now coupled with an elaborate and tedious background of bocage
and were often made to serve as candle-holders with porcelain or gilt-
metal supports rising from the foliage; perched upon pedestals with

heavily scrolled feet, they lost their sense of animation and became more puppetlike.

It is in this setting of lavish table-wares and figures, now intended to be seen only from a frontal view, that we meet the few animals still produced at the Chelsea factory. Francis Barlow's illustrations of *Aesop's Fables* (1st ed., 1666) were still used as a source for animal groups with the backing of the usual bocage, and on the high bases are found the titles of the composition, such as 'The Vain Jack Daw', 'Dog with the Clog', 'The Cock and Jewel', among many others. During this period the usual mark was the bold gold anchor, which, it must be remembered, was also the popular mark for many of the continental reproductions of similar models made in hard-paste porcelain during the second half of the nineteenth century by such firms as Samson of Paris.

In 1758 Sir Everard Fawkener died. After the loss of his patron Sprimont continued as sole proprietor until 1769, when he sold the factory to James Cox and retired. Only two years later, in 1771, he died. The factory was sold by Cox after only one year to William Duesbury and John Heath, proprietors of the Derby factory. The Chelsea works were continued under their direction until 1784. This Chelsea-Derby period was concerned mainly with the manufacture of some of the finest table-wares made in this country during the eighteenth century.

'GIRL-IN-A-SWING' FACTORY OF CHELSEA

In a paper by Arthur Lane and R. J. Charleston read to the English Ceramic Circle on 19 November 1960, chemical analysis was shown to have helped to prove beyond all reasonable doubt that from 1749 until 1754 there were two rival factories working in Chelsea, the later concern probably not actually making saleable wares until 1751. For many years a group of unmarked pieces vaguely similar to Chelsea had worried collectors; the group was generally aligned with an easily identified key piece, the Girl-in-a-Swing, a model of which was given to the Victoria and Albert Museum in 1922 and a further copy of which is in the Museum of Fine Arts, Boston, U.S.A. All the pieces in question were of a very glassy paste, and were found to contain a far greater percentage of lead than the first factory established at Chelsea (averaging over 15 per cent. against the triangle-marked Chelsea of approximately 9 per cent.), all appeared to be the work of a single, and not particularly skilled, modeller. The group illustrated in Plate 19b is from the Alfred Hutton Collection,

IV. CACTUS WREN BY DOROTHY DOUGHTY, WORCESTER (p. 50)

in the Museum of Fine Arts, Boston, and is the only example recorded of this fable group, thought to be based upon an engraving in the *Weekly Apollo*, 1752. This group clearly shows features which when pointed out seem to appear all too obvious, the serrated leaves on the tree-trunk, the crescent-shaped indentations on the upper surface of the base, seemingly made with an impressed finger-nail. Similar features are found on white birds mounted on easily identified bevelled hexagonal bases, which are constantly used by this factory.

The glaze on the Girl-in-a-Swing groups appears to fit the paste much more tightly than on wares from the accepted Chelsea factory, adding clarity of detail to such features as the eyes. The factory appears to have had a large proportion of 'wasters' however, probably from the high lead content causing excessive fire-cracking and collapsing of pieces in the kiln, and consequently about ten inches is the limit to the height of any of their creations. The importance of such documentary pieces as the Fox and the Crane group was certainly not foreseen when a trade account of a dealer in 1770 lists what is thought to be a Bow basket and '2 fox and Crane pieces. o.6.o.' (six shillings?). There has been a lot of doubt cast as to the accuracy of many statements made by Simeon Shaw in his *History of Staffordshire Potteries*, but it seems reasonable to accept his story that the 'breakaway' factory was started by a group of the Staffordshire workers who were recruited by Sprimont to help establish his own factory about 1745. These people would certainly have had a good knowledge of the technique of slip-casting (as described under Techniques), such as was necessary to produce the fine small hollow scent-bottles, seals, snuff-boxes, étuis and trinkets which followed later. These are described in the auctions of the period as Porcelain Toys, and it is fairly evident that Sprimont's Chelsea factory never made such pieces until after the failure and winding up of the rival factory in 1754. The majority of Chelsea toys would appear to have been made in the gold-anchor period (after 1756), and they again show the skill and versatility of the modellers and decorators at the service of the well-established concern. The toys are often thought to be the work of the skilled modeller Joseph Willems, who was employed by Sprimont from 1754 until 1763.

BOW

The factory of Bow was established in about 1748 at Stratford-le-Bow, Middlesex, in East London. The first patent to make porcelain was taken out in 1744 by Edward Heylyn, a Bow merchant, and Thomas Frye, a painter and engraver from Ireland, but no results are known as a consequence of this partnership. In 1749 Frye alone took out a further patent for a material using a high percentage of bone-ash. The first proprietor was Alderman George Arnold, who was succeeded in 1750 by Messrs Weatherby and Crowther, with Frye as manager.

Chelsea had so based their wares on the fashionable continental factories that little originality was left, but with early figures of such popular actors of the day as Henry Woodward, Kitty Clive, David Garrick, and Peg Woffington, Bow can well be considered the most topical London factory. The wares of Bow were obviously intended to cater for less wealthy customers than Chelsea, they aimed at producing good practical useful wares, not lavishly or expensively decorated, and their early figures all appear to be the work of a single modeller.

The paste of Bow during the first five or six years of production is a fine creamy soft-paste porcelain, similar to the paste of the French factory of Saint-Cloud, but in this same period the factory was seemingly constantly experimenting with a variety of glazes, which sometimes makes quick recognition rather difficult.

The lion illustrated in Plate 21a is a rare example of early Bow; a certain attribution was not easy, for the material appears to be slightly higher fired and more of a mass than is customary. It is of interest to see how closely the Bow model follows the original, illustrated in the lower picture (Plate 21b). This marble figure is of early classical date and is situated at the bottom of the steps of the Loggia dei Lanzi, in Florence, and a further lion was carved to make a facing pair in about 1600 by Flaminio Vacca. The figure of the lion is very heavily potted and made in the press-moulded fashion as used at Bow.

In the succeeding period of 1754 to about 1760 the paste of Bow was improved and a soft waxen-like glaze was generally used. The palette included several easily identified colours peculiar to the factory, such as a bright translucent green, which is apt to 'pile up', a soft pastel opaque blue and a strong rose-purple (especially used in '*famille-rose*' reproductions); gilding when used was rather soft and dull, with a tendency to wear off quickly. By about 1755 the simple mound-bases gave way to an increasing use of rococo scrollwork, as illustrated on the figures of the Hen and Cock (Plate 23b). In the early 1760s a characteristic four-footed pedestal was favoured which only served to give a precariously balanced look to the figures and destroyed their animation. Of a similar date to the

Hen and Cock are some charming smaller figures of hounds, hares, and monkeys, often depicted in amusing postures.

The birds made at this London factory were doubtless inspired by Meissen, but while Chelsea endeavoured to faithfully copy the colours of George Edwards, the engraver whose prints they used, Bow painters set out to make a gay composition with clear, bold, and fantastic colouring more appropriate to Birds of Paradise. The fine pair of Tawny Owls in the Schreiber Collection at the Victoria and Albert Museum, and so often illustrated, are typical of such treatment.

During this period Bow and other major English porcelain factories were making tureens in the form of partridges sitting on their nests, and these figures were painted in more sombre naturalistic colours. According to papers left by John Bowcocke the clerk to the Bow factory, he had occasion to purchase 'a partridge alive or dead', which might well have been to provide the modeller of such tureens with a true model.

In 1762 Weatherby died, leaving John Crowther as the sole proprietor, but in the following year he was declared bankrupt. Financial help was obviously forthcoming, for the factory continued until 1775 or 1776, when it was sold to William Duesbury, who removed the moulds to his Derby factory. It is surmised, without any evidence, that it was Duesbury who financed the Bow undertaking during its last stages. From 1763 a regular factory mark seems to have been adopted and appears on both useful wares and figures, giving the title 'anchor and dagger' to this period. The two devices were drawn in a reddish-brown enamel and are sometimes the subject of sharp practice; by removing the dagger with acid, an anchor remains which could well be mistaken by new collectors for the red anchor of Chelsea. Pieces of porcelain are often seen with a suspicious-looking patch on the underside of the base where a late mark has been either ground or etched away and a more exciting mark added in an enamel colour. Similarly a gilt flower or other form painted on a base often hides a late and unimportant factory mark, which can easily be exposed, with the application of a household abrasive, to reveal the true manufacturer, and all too often it reads 'Made in Limoges' or 'Austria'.

The last period of Bow was devoted mostly to the manufacture of poor imitations of Chelsea table-wares and also of large figures with distinctive orange-tinted cheeks and an over-blued glaze.

DERBY

The porcelain of Derby has never been so popular with collectors as the wares of some of the other English soft-paste factories such as Chelsea, Bow, or Worcester. This may well be due to the fact that until recent years, the certain attribution of some specimens to this particular factory was difficult.

Among the most interesting examples of Derby porcelain are those produced prior to 1756. Made as if in competition with the well-known 'goat-and-bee' jugs of triangle-period Chelsea are three small jugs, two with the incised letter D and the date, '1750', while the third bears the word 'Derby'. The man considered responsible for making these and other early examples was Andrew Planché. Although of Huguenot parentage, Planché was born in London in 1728 and apprenticed to a London goldsmith from 1740 to 1747. The registration of the birth of a son shows him to have been at Derby by 1751 at the latest, when he was noted to be a 'China Maker'.

The early groups of figures are now generally accepted as having been made between 1750 and 1755, prior to the establishment in 1756 of the true Derby factory that was to continue until 1848. These early pieces bear no recognized factory mark and it is only on the evidence of constantly recurring features in their construction and material that they are separated as a group. The boar (Plate 20a) is probably the best known of this Planché family. The Derby boars are based on the Roman marble copy of a lost Hellenistic original which was formerly in the Medici Collection. The Roman copy is now in the Uffizi Gallery in Florence (Plate 20b), and there is a further small bronze replica of early seventeenth-century date by Antoni Susini in the Victoria and Albert Museum. The original Derby examples of the 'Florentine Boars' illustrate the pointers to this group; the 'dry edge' around the base which suggests that after being dipped in the glaze a narrow margin was wiped free to prevent the risk of 'tears' forming and fusing the figures to the floor or shelf of the kiln during the firing (in some Chelsea pieces grinding has been necessary to remove such irregularities); secondly, the peculiar funnel-shaped hole in the base already discussed under 'Technique and Materials' and finally the 'slip-cast' method by which all these pieces were made.

The paste of the so-called 'dry edge' family is very rich and creamy in appearance, but sometimes marred by the too-thick, glassy glaze. It is appropriate to mention here a very dangerous class of fakes of boars, other animals, and birds made about 1950–60. They are of a rather poor chalky material with a waxen-like glaze, and are often lightly decorated in a palette which includes an unpleasant fleshy-pink.

Among the other animals made in this early period are sheep, goats, bulls, and stags. There are a pair of 'charging bulls' in the collection of the Derby Museum, painted in the palette attributed to William Duesbury, while he was still working as only a decorator. Arthur Lane notes that these bulls are from engravings after Elias Ridinger and that similar figures also exist in Meissen porcelain. It is interesting to observe that the simple mound bases of the bulls, and similar groups of a seated Doe and a Stag at Lodge, rely upon painted flowers for decoration in preference to the more customary flowers and leaves applied in relief in the Meissen tradition. The dog, Trump (Plate 24c), also has this similar treatment.

The names of Andrew Planché, John Heath the financial backer, and William Duesbury all feature in a draft agreement dated 1 January 1756; this agreement was never executed and later in the year Heath and Duesbury alone were named as the 'Proprietors of the DERBY PORCELAIN Manufactory' and offered at a four-day sale in London, 'A curious collection of fine Figures', etc, 'after the finest Dresden models'. It is apparent that it was the intention of the partners to use the fame of the Meissen factory to popularize their wares, and in 1757 another advertisement refers to 'Derby or second Dresden'. The partners must have been unduly optimistic and could only have hoped that their customers would have seen little of the real German porcelain, for their hybrid paste was very light in weight and chalky, while the intense blueing of the glaze to give the illusion of a hard-paste porcelain was so overdone that flesh tints took on a ghostly pallor.

During the third period of the factory from about 1758 until 1770 the unpleasant blued glaze over a chalky paste dwindles in favour of a creamier white body with a clear colourless glaze. During this period another constantly recurring feature in manufacture found on both figures and on some useful wares helps to identify otherwise unmarked pieces. The wares of this so-called 'patch family' are marked on the bases with three or more patches of dark, unglazed porcelain, caused by the small pads or balls of clay upon which the figures or wares were supported in the kiln during the glazing stage; this feature continued over a long period. The styles of this phase of Derby modelling were much dictated by the fashion of 'gold-anchor' Chelsea, which were, of course, being made under the influence of mid-eighteenth-century Meissen. Animals rarely seem to have been modelled alone, but are certainly featured in some of the more ambitious Derby groups. Europa and the Bull, Leda and the Swan, and the placid leopard with the child on its back (Plate 22a) are fine examples of this period, unspoilt by the popular rococo bases to follow.

During the time that Chelsea and Derby were both under the control of Duesbury (1770–84) great improvements were made in paste and palette. While the production of exceptionally fine useful wares appears to have been the main aim, many figure subjects were still made, with an increasing number being left in the 'biscuit', a fashion popularized by Sèvres. It is of interest to note that these unglazed groups were more expensive than the same model fully glazed and decorated; this was due to the fact that to be sold in the 'biscuit' a piece had to come from the kiln unblemished, whereas glaze and decoration could always be used to remedy slight defects where necessary.

Late in the eighteenth century Derby made reproductions of the popular Meissen group The Tailor and his companion on Goats, modelled by Kaendler and Eberlein, but there is no foundation for the story suggesting that these were made in Meissen originally to fulfil a promise to the Court Tailor that he and his wife should be present at a Court function. The Derby price list describes them as 'Welch Taylor and Family'. The publication by John Haslem, *The Old Derby China Factory*, London, 1876 (Haslem), is of especial interest, for it includes a price list of Derby figures, together with their size and number, which is generally incised under the base of wares made from about 1775.

In 1814 the factory of Derby was purchased by Robert Bloor, who became insane in 1828, but from 1814 until 1848 the term 'Bloor period' is in general usage. The Royal Crown Derby Porcelain Company of today was not established until 1876.

LONGTON HALL

Until the recent publication of the monograph by Dr Bernard Watney devoted to this factory there was a great deal of difference of opinion among the collectors in identifying the productions of this Staffordshire factory. It is a surprising fact that although North Staffordshire has been the centre of the ceramic industry in this country since about 1600, Longton Hall appears to be the only factory in those parts to take up the manufacture of porcelain during the middle of the eighteenth century. The potters of these towns had worked for so many generations on the various forms of earthenware and stoneware that it is very apparent that they found it difficult to adapt themselves to working in this new unfamiliar material and were unable to compete with the high standard set by such contemporary concerns as Chelsea and Worcester.

The name most familiar to us when talking of Longton Hall is that of William Littler, who is best known for the potting of salt-glazed stoneware, especially when decorated with the fine rich blue glaze with added gilt and white enamel. The man who was responsible for the establishment of the factory was a William Jenkinson, who in 1753 sold his shares to a Nathaniel Firmin. From 1755 yet another partner was working with Littler, Robert Charlesworth, who came along with sufficient financial aid to get the concern out of debt, enabling it to flourish for a further five years, when against the wishes of Littler he dissolved the partnership. In September 1760 there was a sale at Salisbury, Wiltshire, at which the factory's stock of 90,000 pieces was disposed of. It is again only recently that information in the form of a headed bill has proved that soon after the closure of Longton Hall, William Littler moved to Scotland, and from 1764 until about 1770 he was working as a 'China maker' at West Pans near Musselburgh. From pieces now identified it seems that he merely added decoration to outmoded and slightly faulty pieces rescued from the old Longton Hall stock to local order, and so far it has been impossible to identify any wares made by him such as those suggested on the bill.

In 1929 Mrs Donald MacAlister, a founder member of the English Ceramic Circle, suggested that an early group of figures, referred to as 'snowmen', might well belong to the Longton Hall factory. The keen observation of this lady has since proved correct, for excavations from the actual site produced part of a figure of a bird and a factory waster of a pug-dog with similarities to the known group of about thirty models so obvious as to leave no doubt. This early group now fall into a distinct class, identified by a thick glaze of almost pure glass containing a mass of small bubbles; the thick glaze is very apt to pile up and craze (minute cracking of the glaze), and the modelling thus takes on a very blurred, but not unpleasing appearance. Most of the models recorded have been modelled after Chinese, Meissen, or Chelsea porcelain originals, some also being found in the lead-glazed earthenware or salt-glazed stoneware of Staffordshire. The figure of a heron from the Rous Lench Collection (Plate 24b), made between 1749 and 1753, is a beautiful example of these figures. Well worthy of mention also is a typical German pug-dog dated 1750 from the same collection, and a taper-holder in the form of a crane in the Victoria and Albert Museum.

From 1754 until 1757, the middle period, there was an improvement in both the material and the quality of the modelling. In this period is found once again the so-called 'Mops', the popular German dog discussed under Meissen animals, but now decorated with splashes of underglaze manganese, giving a purplish-brown colour, and having a gilt collar. This is sometimes found to bear one of the few acknowledged marks of this factory, what could well be a 'J' and 'L' crossed, probably for 'Jenkinson' and 'Longton'. Meissen was again used as a source for the very fine equestrian groups featuring the Turkish or Blackamoor groom modelled by Kaendler (a Meissen original of this group is shown in Plate 12).

The period from 1757 until the closure of the factory in 1760 seems to have been mostly taken up with the production of table-wares. The love of horse modelling, however, is still apparent in what must be one of the finest original models to come from this factory, the Duke of Brunswick (Plate 23a), mounted on a galloping charger, and wearing the Insignia of the Order of the Garter, with which he was invested in 1759. This is one of the last of such important pieces made at this unique factory.

WORCESTER

It appears to be a fact among collectors of porcelain that even if certain models are not of a high quality, providing they are rare, they become important as collectors' pieces and command very high prices in the sale rooms. This especially is the case with the rare Worcester figures.

Worcester has the pride of being the only English porcelain factory established during the middle of the eighteenth century that is still in full production today. The Worcester factory was born at Bristol, at a small factory established in 1749 by William Miller and Benjamin Lund (the old term Lowdin's Bristol has been found to be incorrect). This concern was taken over in 1752, one year after the establishment of the 'Worcester Tonquin Manufacture' at Warmstry House, Worcester in 1751; fifteen gentlemen signed the articles, among them the well-known Dr Wall and William Davis. Dr Wall died in 1776, and William Davis, an apothecary, continued until his own death in 1783, when the factory was sold to Thomas Flight, the firm's London agent, who purchased the concern for his two sons Joseph and John. It is considered today more logical to refer to the 1751–83 period as the First Period, rather than the 'Dr Wall Period'.

The porcelain made at Worcester was a great advance on that of rival factories, for it contained 30–40 per cent. of soap-rock (steatite) from

Cornwall, and the factory assured its customers that the wares would withstand hot water. The porcelain had a fine tight-fitting glaze, often blued to overcome the creamy colour of the paste; it very rarely crazed, and so it was an ideal material for the main production of this prolific factory, which was table-wares.

The few figures made during the eighteenth century at Worcester were late productions and it is 1771 before we have two eyewitness accounts of figure-making at this factory. Mrs Philip Lybbe Powys and Dr Joseph Roche, R.N., both describe their visits to the factory, the latter going so far as to note that the press-moulded technique was used. Only eight models of figures are so far recorded, three pairs, Sportsman, Turk, and Gardener, with their feminine counterparts, a nursing mother, and the Kingfisher as illustrated in Plate 24a. It is very doubtful whether the bird is original to Worcester, for a similar model is known both at Longton Hall and in raised-anchor Chelsea. The figures of Worcester are unmarked and their attribution was made primarily on the amount of soapstone found in the paste.

As previously observed, during the eighteenth century the Worcester porcelain factory made very few figures and even fewer animals or birds, but this has been remedied during this century by the fine series of birds they have produced.

It is rare for artists in porcelain to have achieved such success in their lifetime as that won by Dorothy Doughty, the modeller of a splendid series of Audubon's 'Birds of America'. Modelled for the Worcester Royal Porcelain Company Ltd, since 1935, in limited editions, the demand has always outrun the supply. These birds are more than a pretty piece of porcelain; they are faithfully produced in detail, coupled with the plants, flowers and other insect and animal life with which the bird is generally associated and the group is formed to give a pleasing view from any angle.

The artist entrusted by the company with this costly and daring enterprise was the daughter of Charles Doughty, the traveller and poet. It was in 1933 that work started on the first productions. Soon it was found necessary to work from live birds rather than museum specimens in order to capture the essential vitality. The first models (Redstarts on Hemlock), an edition of sixty-six, were the only pair of figures made from paintings and photographs.

In 1950 the second series of American birds was issued and success was achieved, after many painstaking efforts, in illustrating the birds in flight. In 1953 and 1956 the Worcester Company arranged for Miss Doughty to go to America to make detailed studies of yet further birds. The Cactus Wren (Colour Plate IV) was modelled from life in Tucson, Arizona; the surrounding country is inhabited with mountain lions, wild deer, wild pigs, and many deadly reptiles, and the wren has the reputation of giving the alarm at the presence of a snake and so the Coral Snake is included in the group illustrated.

The material used is bone-china. The first firing stage calls for a very elaborate system of propping, each individual prop being so placed not only to support a particular section of the model at the critical firing temperature, but also to fall away when it has completed its job. After the glaze has been fired the figures often have as many as six or seven further firings before all the matt enamel colours have been added. Due to their wide popularity in America, these figures are already regarded as collectors' items and change hands for several times their original cost.

LOWESTOFT

The factory of Lowestoft, Suffolk, was established in 1757 and continued in production until 1802, when the proprietors appear to have taken an interest in the more lucrative trade of herring curing. The paste of Lowestoft is almost identical to that of Bow and there is a colourful story telling that Robert Browne, a Lowestoft partner, had previously taken employment at the Bow factory in order to learn the secrets of porcelain manufacture.

This Suffolk factory was devoted almost entirely to simple, but pleasing, useful wares decorated in underglaze blue in both Chinese and Worcester styles and also enamelled wares painted in a distinctive palette influenced by both Worcester and late Meissen flower painting. There are in addition many interesting documentary examples, such as in the collection of the Norwich Castle Museum, which were especially made to order as commemorative pieces.

Well worthy of note for the purposes of this volume are the delightful small figures of cats, sheep, and swans. The cats and the sheep generally have green enamelled bases, while the swans have beaks of a distinctive orange-red; such models have been identified by moulds found on the site, but single attribution is difficult and comparison with pieces in public collections is desirable.

ROCKINGHAM

The factory at Swinton, South Yorkshire, now more widely known as Rockingham, was first established soon after the middle of the eighteenth century, and at this time the wares had much in common with those being produced in Staffordshire during the same period. It was not until 1826 that the fine high-quality bone-china porcelain was being made in sufficient quantities to market.

Rockingham made some beautifully finished services and vases from this date and was even patronized by King William IV, but a great many wares have been attributed to this factory without any grounds whatever. A recent publication throws a great deal of new light on the wares of this popular factory, *The Rockingham Pottery*, by A. E. Eaglestone and T. A. Lockett (Municipal Museum and Art Gallery, Rotherham), 1964. It lists over sixty of the marked series of one hundred and twenty figures considered to have been made at Rockingham, and included in the list are over twenty animal groups of rabbits, dogs, squirrels, cats, stags, hinds, sheep, and rams. It will be disappointing news to the many collectors of 'Rockingham poodles' that there is no evidence among these identified pieces to suggest that any 'rough-coated' animals were ever made at the Rockingham factory, which closed in 1842.

PLYMOUTH AND BRISTOL

The two porcelain factories of the West Country and the names associated with their establishment are always conveniently grouped as one, i.e. Plymouth and Bristol of Cookworthy and Champion. The claim to fame of this particular concern was that it was the first English factory to produce true hard-paste porcelain.

William Cookworthy (b. 1705, d. 1780) was a Quaker and chemist from Plymouth, who had for a long time been interested in discovering the whereabouts of the essential ingredients required for making true porcelain in this country. Cookworthy was acquainted with the writings of Père d'Entrecolles, the Jesuit missionary who had witnessed the production of porcelain in China at Ching-tê Chên and had described their methods. Some time prior to 1768 Cookworthy had located deposits of both china-clay and china-stone near St Austell in Cornwall and in that year the 'Plymouth New Invented Patent Porcelain Manufactory' was established. This factory was transferred to Bristol in 1770 and in 1773 Cookworthy, who was then 68 years old, sold his patent to Richard Champion. Two years later, when Champion applied for an extention of the Patent, he was opposed by a group of Staffordshire potters, including Josiah Wedgwood, who wished to include these newly found materials in their own wares. The result was that while Champion was permitted to retain his patent for the manufacture of porcelain, his rivals were allowed the use of china-clay and china-stone in opaque earthenware and stoneware.

The production at Plymouth and Bristol experienced many difficulties, due to the fact that as they used a smaller proportion of the fusible china-stone in their mixture than either the Chinese or Germans they had to fire their wares to an even higher temperature. A great deal of smoke-staining in the glaze is often present, together with fire-cracking and warping, and the figures have a tendency to lean out of true. The enamel colours, which lie too obviously on the surface of the glaze, often flake off.

The alchemist sign for tin, the so-called '2–4' mark, was used at Ply-mouth, while a cross or 'B' appears on wares made at Bristol, but only on useful wares, for it seemed to be the practice to leave figures unmarked.

The early days at Plymouth were devoted mainly to the production of table-wares and only about twenty-varieties of figures are recorded, most of these appear to have been made up from moulds which had been used formerly at the Staffordshire factory of Longton Hall, which had closed eight years earlier.

It is difficult to separate the figures of Plymouth and Bristol with any certainty; the alert-looking hare (Plate 22b) is considered to have been made at Plymouth. The elusive repairer-modeller Mr Tebo is thought to have been associated with Bristol between 1772 and November 1774. The impressed mark 'T' or 'To' appears on Bow figures, ornamental wares, and the rare figures of Worcester, and on vases and shell-shaped salts of Bristol. Tebo is thought to have had a French name such as Thibaud, and he was presumably a 'repairer' responsible for assembling the various cast or pressed sections of complicated wares and figures. There is proof that he attempted to model at times, for in 1775 'Mr Tebo' was at Etruria in Staffordshire working for Josiah Wedgwood, who writes in despair to his partner Bentley, 'Mr Tebo has had a cast of a Hare's Head before him some time, *but it is not a likeness.* The wet plaister in casting presses down the hair upon the face, and makes it look more like the head of a drown'd puppy, and Mr Tebo cannot model anything like the face of a Hare—he has made many attempts at sundry times, but they generally turn out to be full as like pigs as Hares.' On this evidence the hare illustrated must certainly have been made at Plymouth or Bristol without the aid of Mr Tebo.

Among the other animals and birds made here in this new material were nicely modelled lions and lionesses, sheep, cows, goats, and dogs, while pheasants and finches appear to have been the most popular among the birds; when coloured, most exotic tints were used, including a very strong vermilion which is indicative of the Plymouth works.

After losing the sole right of using china-clay and china-stone, Champion appears to have lost his enthusiasm for the wares which he had claimed had the hardness of Dresden and the elegance of Sèvres. In 1778 a Commission in Bankruptcy was declared against him, but temporarily suspended, and he left Bristol in 1781 to establish a company in Staffordshire. This move resulted in the formation of the New Hall factory, but Champion was concerned only until the following year, when he ceased to have interests in the production of porcelain. The New Hall factory continued to make useful wares in hard-paste porcelain until about 1812, when the material was abandoned in favour of the more popular bone-china.

English Earthenwares

IN THE LIGHT of recent research, classes of English pottery dating back to Saxon times have been identified, but throughout these early centuries it was rare for the country potter serving the needs of his immediate locality to make any identifiable wares other than those for kitchen and building purposes. Exceptional are the water-vessels of the twelfth to thirteenth centuries; these amusing jugs or aquamaniles were often made in the form of stags, rams, or equestrian figures, they poured from the mouth of the animal and are thought to have been used to wash the hands between courses.

Other rare early animal forms are the simple cats and dogs of tin-glazed earthenware made by the 'galley-potters' of London, they often bear dates around 1675 and the cats are sometimes depicted as tabbies with the markings in high-temperature colours of cobalt and manganese.

From the early seventeenth century until today North Staffordshire has been the accepted centre of the English pottery industry; the geographical conditions were ideal, there was ample suitable clay, unlimited supplies of coal for fuel, and near-by ports, later assisted by canals for water transport. The earthenwares of Staffordshire and other seventeenth-century centres such as Wrotham, Kent, were again devoted to normal domestic wares and it was only occasionally that an unusually lavish dish or posset-pot would be made to a special order to mark the occasion of a birth, wedding, or some other commemorative event. It was the early years of the eighteenth century before earthenware figures began to be made for a purely decorative rather than functional purpose. The important salt-glazed stoneware figures of John Dwight of Fulham made during the last quarter of the seventeenth century are more appropriate to the art of the sculptor.

In the face of such competition as that of the Elers brothers, the Staffordshire potter seems suddenly to have become aware that if he were to survive then he must improve upon the 'peasant pottery' that he had continued to produce with little technical improvement for over fifty years. It became necessary to 'tidy up' his old-worldly crude wares and make them more attractive to a wider market.

In his search for the secret of manufacturing porcelain John Dwight had improved upon the coarse grey stonewares of Germany with the addition of calcined flints. By some undiscovered means, this process soon became known to the potters of Staffordshire and resulted in fine salt-glazed stonewares being produced in about 1720. It was in this new material that the Staffordshire potters first started to make figures to be hawked around the countryside and sold at weekly markets and fairs. Among the first such animals to be reproduced were models of the familiar household pets and the animals of the farmyard. The smug fire-side cat was a particular favourite made in solid agate-ware. To obtain the agate or marbled effect, clays of varying colours, generally white and brown, were 'wedged' together to give the appearance of 'strata'. They were then cut and rolled into thin slabs to be hand-pressed into the walls of a simple two-piece mould. Occasionally the clay was artificially stained blue with cobalt to produce yet another colour, but this strong oxide sometimes gives an overall blue tinge to the entire work. Such wares obviously could not be made by the 'slip-cast' method, because of the need for keeping the colours clearly defined, the glazing was carried out by the normal high-temperature salt-glazed method.

The pug illustrated in Plate 25a is a less common example of a whole range of similar animals made in salt-glazed stoneware by the usual method of 'slip-casting'. Use was often made of high-temperature oxide colouring to give a little variation to such wares; cobalt was the most common and the wares which were decorated by having the incised pattern or details filled with this colour are called 'scratch blue'. The use of manganese, as for the eyes of the pug, was less common.

The animals associated with the popular sport of hunting naturally commanded attention, and so the fox, stag, hind, hare, and rabbit are all featured about this time in salt-glazed stoneware.

Staffordshire was certainly not alone in the production of salt-glazed stoneware and many models were also made at both Nottingham and Derby. Among them are the amusing beer-mugs in the form of bears sitting up on their haunches clasping a terrier in a fatal hug, with, as in the later Sussex pigs, the head detachable to form a cup (Plate 25b). These were made over quite a long period from the middle of the eighteenth century. The relaxed greyhounds which are far more common were made chiefly at Brampton and at Chesterfield, in Derby during the first quarter of the nineteenth century. In both of these cases the drab colour of the clay is often enriched by brushing it over, sometimes only partially, with a slip rich in iron which when fired gives a warm metallic brown. Among the many jugs and bowls made at Nottingham during the first half of the eighteenth century are some rather wooden-looking hawks with incised decoration, which are also generally stained to a dark copper-brown.

In addition to such familiar animals the Staffordshire potters attempted to imitate the continental porcelain factories and model wild animals which they had probably only heard of at second hand or seen illustrated. A well-known class of monkeys with their young was a favourite model.

By the middle of the eighteenth century the Staffordshire salt-glaze potters became aware of the threat to their living from the increased production of English porcelain, and so they endeavoured to rival this new body in decoration by adding enamel colours to the salt-glaze body. It is in this field that the decorator William Duesbury is again encountered. Among the wares attributed to his workshop are some charming groups of ewes with lambs; they lie on a mound before a tree in a very porcelain-like grouping and the entire surface is painted in coloured enamels. The painting of some swans and cygnets leaves little doubt as to the identity of painter, for in the notebooks of William Duesbury the entry is found '*swimming swans donn all over*'.

In addition to the salt-glazed stonewares the Staffordshire potters continued to produce the traditional lead-glazed wares, but in a more refined material and workmanlike finish than previously. One of the first English potters to lend his name to such wares was John Astbury (b. 1686, d. 1743), of Shelton, near Hanley. Astbury is associated with two important developments which were stepping-stones to the improvement of the wares of the Staffordshire potter; one was the introduction of white Devonshire clays as a 'top dressing' to normal red-wares, and the second was the use of calcined flints to give both whiteness and hardness to a cream-coloured body.

These so-called 'Astbury' wares relied solely on the use of various-coloured clays to give them interest. Although dull when first fired, the clays took on a deep richness when covered with a honey-coloured lead-glaze. By about 1740 a new method of dipping the biscuited wares in a liquid glaze resulted in a far more even and thinner glaze finish. The majority of 'Astbury' figures are in human form, topers and musicians, but in collections throughout the country there are a large number of very fine mounted cavalrymen. Similar figures were certainly made up to fairly recent times to deceive the purchaser, but they are usually of a softer material.

The amusing owl (Plate 26c) is an uncommon model showing the use of the still popular seventeenth-century slipware technique of 'feathering' the contrasting bands of coloured slip by means of a pointed tool. The tool is dragged across the lines of wet slip at more or less equal intervals to obtain the effect of feathering; in this instance it is very appropriate and looks far more suitable than when used as yet another form of decoration on the many posset-pots where the potter often tends to overdecorate by using every trick-of-the-trade.

The outstanding potter associated with some of the finest of Staffordshire figures is undoubtedly Thomas Whieldon of Little Fenton. It was Whieldon to whom Josiah Wedgwood became a junior partner in 1754, remaining there until he started his own pottery in about 1759. From the middle of the eighteenth century there was a noticeable improvement in the quality of the cream-coloured clays. The white body which was normally used for salt-glazed wares could be kept to a lower temperature, resulting in a porous body that required the protection of a lead-glaze. It was this slightly yellow glaze, which was applied by dipping, that Whieldon used to such advantage in his 'tortoiseshell' and mottled coloured glazes (Plates 26a and b). Although obviously inspired by Chinese, Meissen, and English porcelain originals, Whieldon made no attempt to imitate these finer wares. His technique consisted of staining his glazed wares before firing with patches of various metallic oxides, giving the usual range of blues, greens, yellows, and browns as previously described. As with 'Astbury' wares, there is little doubt that other neighbouring potters quickly made use of a similar finish for their wares.

It is regrettable that Whieldon never used a factory mark, but following excavations on the site of his potworks at Fenton certain classes of high-quality wares can be attributed to him with very little doubt. The Chinese *blanc-de-chine* figures that had been made in China from the seventeenth century were obviously well known in England by the middle of the eighteenth century; they were used as models at Lund and Miller's Bristol factory, and a fragment from a similar deity was found on the Fenton site. There are many Whieldon examples known of the water-buffalo with the perky little boy on his back taken from a Chinese original, while the well-known crested bird is remarkably similar to both Meissen and Chelsea pieces. A whole group of more naïve animals and birds must have been the original work of the modeller, and many such rare examples are in the Rous Lench and Colonial Williamsburg collections.

Josiah Wedgwood's main aim appears to have been a complete

breakaway from any material or style that was associated with traditional Staffordshire wares, and so apart from the rare figures of birds, mythical animals such as sphinxes and griffins, and hedgehogs perforated with holes for growing crocuses, his fine stonewares of the eighteenth century were used only for good table-wares and reproductions of classical vases. From the nineteenth century figures of small animals and fox-head stirrup-cups became more common. A whole series of animals such as gazelles, monkeys, panthers, and sea-lions were made in earthenware and modelled by John Skeaping from about 1930, and there are very few ceramic enthusiasts who are not acquainted with the lovely bull decorated with Signs of the Zodiac modelled for Wedgwoods in 1945 by Arnold Machin.

Wedgwood, of course, had many imitators both in style and material, but there were still a number of well-established potters in Staffordshire who continued to cater for what must have been a diminishing market.

Many of the figures made by Ralph Wood of Burslem (b. 1715, d. 1772). bear the impressed mark of 'R. Wood' or 'Ra. Wood Burslem', and so with surviving lists it is possible to establish beyond doubt many of Wood's productions. The outstanding difference in the wares of Whieldon and Wood is in the behaviour of the coloured glazes. Whieldon made little attempt to colour his wares in a normal manner, probably because he found it too difficult. He seemingly preferred to dab on his colours and let the natural running of the glassy glaze during the firing take over, with, as is now admitted, great success. Whieldon's rare attempts to actually place colours in a logical manner, as on his copy of a Kaendler Turk, may well be quoted as a disaster.

Ralph Wood chose to colour his figures by actually brushing on the stained glaze in the appropriate hue as far as the limited range of high-temperature colours would permit. In Plate 27a this process is seen to have been remarkably successful and the colours have remained almost exactly where intended. Another fine figure in which Wood had equal success is the popular Sir Hudibras mounted on his pathetic nag, a group derived from an engraving by William Hogarth for an illustrated edition of Samuel Butler's poem published in 1726. It is Ralph Wood, of course, who is credited with the introduction of the famous Toby Jug, based this time on a well-known Yorkshire toper who was pictured on a ballad-sheet of 1761.

In addition to such large and important groups, Ralph Wood, together with his son Ralph (d. 1795), made a large number of simpler wares such as shown on Plate 27b, but of such perfection that they have a beauty unmatched by porcelain. The younger Ralph Wood did not continue to make wares decorated with high-temperature colours for long after the death of his father. Probably on economic grounds, he changed to dipping the now almost white body into a slightly blued, clear glaze, which after firing was decorated with enamel colours in the usual porcelain fashion. The figures made in this period were almost entirely of human forms, particularly busts, catering for the new taste for Classicism, a style for which such material was poorly suited.

Although the general use of high-temperature colours for decoration went out of fashion for a period in about 1780, the continued use of this style by Felix Pratt of Fenton and a few other potters has resulted in the adoption of the term 'Pratt ware'. This generally features high-relief moulded decoration picked out in rather muddy shades of blue, green, and orange on a large variety of jugs, vases, and miscellaneous wares. The same term is applied to pieces of normal 'thrown' shapes when a similar range of colours is used. There are some very finely modelled figures of cocks and hens painted in this style, dating from 1790–1800 and referred to as 'Pratt type'.

During the time of Whieldon noticeable advances were made towards perfecting a good earthenware which would be acceptable by the fastidious buyer as an alternative to the more expensive porcelain. This cream-coloured earthenware body was not confined to Staffordshire alone and the wares made at the Yorkshire factory of Leeds deserve great appreciation in their own right, rather than as a 'poor relation' of Josiah Wedgwood's 'Queen's ware'.

The most important creamware factory in Yorkshire was the Leeds Pottery, established shortly before 1758. The earliest wares produced at this factory were for the table and the shapes had much in common with salt-glazed stoneware, redware, and 'Whieldon'-type earthenware, which they continued to make. Creamwares in these forms however, soon gave way to shapes more fitting to the finer material.

In about 1790 the Leeds Pottery started to manufacture creamware figures; the earliest were of a simple type, again more associated with salt-glaze models, such as pew groups, but later figures such as Venus, Neptune, Bacchus, and Minerva were produced much in the style of the Derby porcelain. Birds and animals were also made at this time, sometimes decorated with splashes of green or yellow underglaze colouring, and in this group are some pleasing figures of foxes and farmyard birds.

The most prized possession of any creamware collector would be a

Leeds horse; these models, judging by the varying materials in which they appear, were seemingly made over a long period. The earliest pieces known are in the accepted creamware of early Leeds with the fine pale-yellow glaze, others are recorded in the later creamware or 'pearlware', where the glaze is deliberately blued to give the illusion of a pure white body. The horse illustrated on Plate 28a, from the collection of the Leeds Art Gallery, is of a later date. It is made from a very white earthenware and is decorated in a 'sponged' manner with blue, orange, and black enamels. It has been suggested that this rather late and colourful horse might well have been made in about 1835 elsewhere in Leeds from the moulds used at the Leeds Pottery, which had become bankrupt in 1820.

From the beginning of the nineteenth century social and economic upheavals throughout the whole country gave birth to a new level of society. People whose entire earnings had previously been spent on the necessities of life were now able to purchase little luxuries that they could not previously afford. With better furnishing of the humble home and farmstead came a demand for colourful ornamentation, and so for people who still could not indulge in the luxury of expensive porcelain figures many Staffordshire factories began to produce comparable figures and groups in earthenware, popularly known as chimney ornaments.

In addition to the large factories such as Wedgwood, Spode, and Minton, a whole cluster of small 'potbanks' quickly sprang into operation, the staff sometimes consisting of merely the potter and a few labourers. Conditions were very primitive and in order to produce competitive wares advantage was taken of cheap child-labour. Documentary reports published in 1842 concerning the employment of children in factories tell of a child working six days a week making as many as two hundred and forty dozen figures for a wage of two shillings a week.

It is known that there were a large number of modellers, but the identification of their individual work is very difficult and so, as in the eighteenth century, the name of one individual whose work can be more readily recognized today is used to refer to a whole group of wares similar in type and thought to be of the same period.

John Walton was such a person. He is thought to have started potting in the first decade of the nineteenth century and he continued until about 1835. Walton's wares were far superior to the 'flat-back' figures which followed the accession of Queen Victoria. He endeavoured to model his earthenwares in the spirit of the finer porcelain of the late eighteenth century and was especially keen on the effect of 'bocage', the tree-like formation used as a background. The majority of Walton type groups depict human forms, such as Biblical characters, shepherds, shepherdesses, fishwives, hunters, gardeners, and Toby jugs, but in addition animals such as the lion, unicorn, cows, sheep, and the camel and dromedary (Plate 28b) were also made at a low cost to garnish the chimney-piece. Walton was one of the few 'toy' makers who marked many of his wares, and the name WALTON, within a scroll or frame is frequently seen on the reverse of his pieces.

Ralph Salt and his son, who worked at Hanley from 1812 until 1864 made wares very similar to those of Walton, and they also marked their pieces in a like manner. Salt often made use of metallic lustres derived from gold and silver to elaborate his work.

Many of the potters who set up their own 'potbanks' soon failed and consequently many of the moulds in use were constantly changing hands, making it almost impossible to suggest a maker for many of the unmarked pieces.

Probably one of the best known nineteenth-century Staffordshire groups is that of the the the bull illustrated in Plate 29a. This large figure is attributed to Obadiah Sherratt, who started the production of earthenware chimney ornaments in Burslem about 1810. After the death of Sherratt about 1840 the pottery was continued by his son and family until some time around 1855. Bull-baiting was one of the many cruel sports practised in Staffordshire until 1835, and this group was undoubtedly a good seller. Another multi-animal group thought to be an early work of Obadiah Sherratt was 'Polito's Menagerie' (Mr Polito died in 1814). It was a very ambitious group for the time, showing the façade of a travelling booth, a 'MENAGERIE OF THE WONDERFUL BIRDS AND BEASTS FROM MOST PARTS OF THE WORLD'. This group, which is twelve inches high, is in the Newcastle under Lyme Museum, and it stands on a typical six-legged platform so often indicative of Sherratt's models. Similar bases support figures of Remus and Romulus being suckled by the wolf, the 'Roran Lion' and 'Mr Munro' being savaged by a tiger in 1792.

The Englishman has the reputation abroad of loving animals more than children, and this was apparently the case in the early nineteenth century, when the general public at least showed such interest in the arrival of a new species of animal to this country, the giraffe. The now world-famous Zoological Gardens at Regent's Park, planned by Decimus Burton, were first opened to the public on 27 April 1828. Probably with the Zoo in mind, the Pasha of Egypt, in August 1827, had presented to George IV a giraffe, accompanied by two Nubian attendants. Despite careful nursing at Windsor Castle, the animal died in August 1829. Public interest in the welfare of this creature had been so great as to justify a caricature by William Heath, under his pseudonym of 'Paul Pry', showing George IV and his unpopular companion Lady Conyngham endeavouring to nurse the sick animal back to health with the aid of a windlass, clothing, and medicine. In 1836 a further small herd was purchased for the Zoo and these giraffes flourished and propagated.

The Staffordshire earthenware figure shown in Plate 30 is still in the tradition of the finer eighteenth-century porcelains, calling for far more skill in the making than the usual figures produced so cheaply in simple moulds by child-labour.

From the early 1840s the figures produced by the numerous model-makers of Staffordshire became both bulky and naive, requiring only a two or three-piece mould for their manufacture. It was at this time that the so-called 'Staffordshire Dogs' first made their appearance. George Hood, James Dudson, and Sampson Smith are among the many potters recorded as having made such models, and the fashion has survived until today. Many of these figures have been made in this century and one of the most prolific manufacturers, William Kent (Porcelains) Ltd, of Burslem, only ceased to make such objects from nineteenth-century moulds in 1962. Deliberate scratching with a file, or other sharp tool, is frequently seen on late Staffordshire models to give the appearance of age, but it should be noted that parallel lines all running in the same direction do not occur in glaze scratched naturally through the years.

All too often the wares of some of the smaller earthenware potteries are either passed over as unimportant or wrongly attributed to one of the many factories of the great Staffordshire industry. Such is the case with the Sussex and Kentish potteries of the late eighteenth and nineteenth centuries. Documented and dated wares of the famous Wrotham potters of Kent are well known from the early seventeenth century, but Sussex pottery is more difficult to identify. Pottery from both of these counties was made of a common red-burning clay covered with rich lead glaze which shows to great advantage the pleasing brownish-black speckling caused by the presence of iron in the clay. This feature is well illustrated in the drinking vessels in the form of pigs from the famous Kidd Collection now housed in Colonial Williamsburg, Virginia, U.S.A. (Plate 29B). These vessels are probably among the best known of all Sussex pottery and must have been in popular use at many convivial farmhouse or inn gatherings. The head, which is detachable, forms a cup which will rest rather precariously on the snout, whilst the headless pig sits comfortably on his haunches. Such pigs have proved so popular that they have remained in production for over one hundred and fifty years. In the more recent models the ears of the pig have been lengthened to enable the cup to stand more safely and the earlier wooden peg used to locate the head in the correct position has been replaced by a special flange which locks into a perforation in the neck of the vessel. Of similar interest and not generally associated with Sussex are whistles in the form of birds. An interesting example in the Hastings Museum, which is rich in Sussex pottery, is a heavily glazed bird with the feathers inlaid with a different-coloured clay. Writing of such whistles the late Mr Edmund Austin, J.P., of Brede, observed, 'These birds were made with a whistle in the tail. They were often built into old farmhouse chimneys, so that when the wind blew, the bird whistled, which was thought to keep evil spirits away—a symbolic survival of the rites of long ago.' The same writer gives an interesting account of the wares made at Brede in East Sussex, where the amusing little hedgehogs were produced during the early nineteenth century purely as ornaments.

In 1815 a new London pottery factory was established which still today numbers its wares among the best of English manufactures; the firm of Doultons was founded at Lambeth. Their early salt-glazed stonewares do not warrant special mention, but in about 1870 came a revival of fine decorative wares and the interest of the ceramic admirers of the day was gained. Apart from the interesting figures by such people as George Tinworth, M. V. Marshall, and L. Harradine, the factory concentrated on jugs, tankards, and vases, illustrating many novel techniques on well-designed shapes.

The only independent or studio potters to make wares similar in style to Doulton were the Martin brothers; these four brothers, Robert Wallace, Charles, Walter, and Edwin, were all born in London between 1843 and 1860. In 1864 Wallace, who showed early promise as a sculptor, was admitted to the Royal Academy School. His close contact with the Lambeth School of Art and the modellers of Doultons' Lambeth factory obviously inspired him in 1873 to set up a pottery studio at King's Road, Fulham, where he and his brothers could work. Both younger brothers, Edwin and Walter, had attended the Lambeth School of Art and gained a certain amount of practical pottery experience as assistants at the Doulton factory. In 1874 the Martin brothers were in business and dated examples of salt-glazed stoneware were fired first in the Fulham kilns of C. J. C. Bailey, and later at a Shepherd's Bush glassworks. New premises were taken over in 1877 at Southall where the brothers could fire their own wares.

The major part of the Martin brothers' output was decorative wares, but Wallace soon took to modelling grotesque birds as illustrated in Plate 31. These 'Alice in Wonderland' creatures were discussed in the 1883 *Art Journal* and through their half-human expressions they seemed to catch the imagination of a large following. They were probably, like many earlier vessels with detachable heads, intended to be used as a container and cup, but who would relish drinking from such an ominous-looking creature? Nevertheless these figures remained a popular line almost to the time the studio closed in 1914.

America

THE FINAL illustration in this book (Plate 32) shows an example of the work of a contemporary modeller Edward Marshall Boehm. Mr Boehm, an American born near Baltimore in Maryland, did not take up ceramic sculpture until he was nearly 40 years of age, although his previous working years spent in animal husbandry had given him a close love and understanding of animals and nature. For many years Mr Boehm had practised sculpture as a hobby only, and it was not until 1949 that he set up a studio at the pottery centre of Trenton, New Jersey, to turn his outstanding ability to commercial advantage.

The American market for such porcelain figures was already well catered for by the English series of American Birds made at the Worcester factory from models by Dorothy Doughty in a bone-china. Edward Marshall Boehm's birds and other animal figures are made from true hard-paste porcelain in the manner of Meissen, but it was not until the Metropolitan Museum of Art, New York, exhibited in their ceramic collections two of his figures, a Hereford Bull, and a Percheron Stallion, that the skill of this artist was fully appreciated and internationally recognized.

As with his English rival, Mr Boehm and his apprentice model only from life and he breeds the necessary wild species depicted in his ceramic creations. The original models are made from a mixture of ball-clay and glycerine (Plasteline), and the model has to be scaled up by about 13 per cent, which is the amount that the finished figure will shrink when fired. The Plasteline model is then cut up and appropriate moulds made (as described under 'Technique'). A plaster version is produced next to be used as a standard figure by the assemblers of the various cast pieces. The rather high figure of thirty-five is given as the life of a Boehm mould; usually with the slip-cast method of production the mould would have started to lose the fine detail of the original before this number had been cast.

The figure of a robin as illustrated was presented to Queen Elizabeth II in 1964 as a gift from the Congressional Club of Washington, D.C. As with their English counterparts, such figures are made only in limited editions, thus creating a seller's market, and in this instance the edition was limited to five hundred.

To have made such an impact with modern porcelain sculpture in such a short time, in face of such a competitive market, is a great accomplishment, and, as long as there are collectors and public galleries who can afford the necessarily high prices charged for these antiques of the future, it is to be hoped that modellers, working in the tradition of the great Kaendler of Meissen, will continue to fulfil the desire of all lovers of pottery and porcelain for the figures of animals and birds.

Bibliography

T. H. Clarke, 'French Influences at Chelsea', *English Ceramic Circle Translations*, Vol. 4, Pt. 5 (1954).

J. P. Cushion, *Handbook of Pottery and Porcelain Marks*, 3rd ed. (Faber, London, 1965).

Siegfried Ducret, *German Porcelain and Faïence* (Oldbourne Press, London, 1962).

F. Brayshaw Gilhespy, *Derby Porcelain* (Macgibbon & Kee, London, 1961).

Reginald Haggar, *Staffordshire Chimney Ornaments* (Phoenix House Ltd, London, 1955).

W. B. Honey, *The Ceramic Art of China* (Faber, London, 1945).

— *Dresden China* (Faber, London, 1954).

— *English Pottery and Porcelain*, 5th ed. (A. & C. Black, London, 1962).

Arthur Lane, *French Faïence* (Faber, London, 1948).

— *Later Islamic Pottery* (Faber, London, 1951).

— *English Porcelain Figures of the 18th Century* (Faber, London, 1961).

George Savage, *French Porcelain* (Barrie & Rockliff, London, 1960).

Donald Towner, *The Leeds Pottery* (Cory, Adams & Mackay, London, 1963).

Hugh Wakefield, *Victorian Pottery* (Herbert Jenkins, London, 1962).

Worcester Royal Porcelain Co Ltd (Appreciation by George Savage), *The American Birds of Dorothy Doughty* (Worcester, 1962).

Index

1. Horse, Chinese, Six Dynasties (p. 11)

2a. Rhinoceros, Chinese, Han Dynasty (p. 10)

2b. Ox-drawn cart, Chinese, about seventh century (p. 11)

3a. Guardian lion, Chinese, Six Dynasties (p. 11)

3b. Sheep in pen, Chinese, Han Dynasty (p. 9)

4a. Lion, Chinese, tenth to eleventh centuries (p. 12)

4b. Kylin (p. 13)

5a. Lion, Japanese, late seventeenth century (p. 15)

5b. Dogs of Fo, Chinese, reign of K'ang Hsi (p. 13)

6a. Horse, Turkish,
nineteenth century (p. 16)

6b. Cat, Persian,
seventeenth century (p. 15)

7a. Hounds, Meissen, about 1740 (p. 22)

7b. Cats, Meissen, about 1740 (p. 22)

8. Vulture, Meissen, dated 1734 (p. 20)

9. Bolognese Hound (p. 19)

10 and 11. Monkey-band by J. J. Kaendler (p. 21)

12. Horse and Blackamoor by Kaendler, Meissen, about 1750 (p. 22)

13. Pelican, by Kaendler in 1732 (p. 20)

15. Horse, Höchst, about 1770 (p. 23)

Bear, Nymphenburg, about 1765 (p. 24)

16a. Lions, Lunéville, about 1775 (p. 32)

16b. Boar, Strasburg, about 1755 (p. 35)

17a. Dog of Madame Pompadour, Vincennes, about 1750 (p. 30)

17b. Hare, St Cloud, about 1750 (p. 28)

18a. Little Hawk Owl, with engraving, Chelsea, about 1752 (p. 36)

18b. Goats, Chelsea, about 1752 (p. 36)

19a. Rabbit, Chelsea, about 1755 (p. 28)

19b. Fox and Crane, Chelsea (Girl-in-a-Swing), about 1751 (p. 40)

20a. Boar, Derby, 1750–5 (p. 44)

20b. Boar, early Roman marble (p. 44)

21a. Lion, Bow, 1750–5 (p. 42)

21b. Lion, early Roman marble (p. 42)

22a. Leopard,
Derby, about
1760 (p. 46)

22b. Hare,
Plymouth,
about 1770
(p. 52)

23a. Equestrian group, Longton Hall, about 1760 (p. 48)

23b. Hen and Cock, Bow, about 1760 (p. 42)

24a. Kingfisher, Worcester, about 1770
(p. 49)

24b. Heron, Longton Hall, about 1750
(p. 47)

24c. Hogarth's dog 'Trump', English, 1750–5 (p. 38)

25a. Pug, Staffordshire, about 1745 (p. 55)

25b. Bears, Staffordshire, mid-eighteenth century (p. 55)

26a. Tiger, Staffordshire, about 1750 (p. 57)

26b. Bird, Staffordshire,
about 1750 (p. 57)

26c. Owl, Staffordshire,
mid-eighteenth century (p. 57)

27a. Elephant, Staffordshire, about 1770 (p. 58)

27b. Stags and Hind, Staffordshire, 1770–5 (p. 58)

28a. Horse, Leeds, about 1835 (p. 60)

28b. Dromedary and Camel, Staffordshire, about 1830 (p. 61)

29a. Bull, Staffordshire, about 1825 (p. 61)

29b. Pigs, Sussex, early nineteenth century (p. 62)

31. Owl by Martin Brothers, Southall, dated 1899 (p. 64

30. Giraffe, Staffordshire, about 1830 (p. 62)

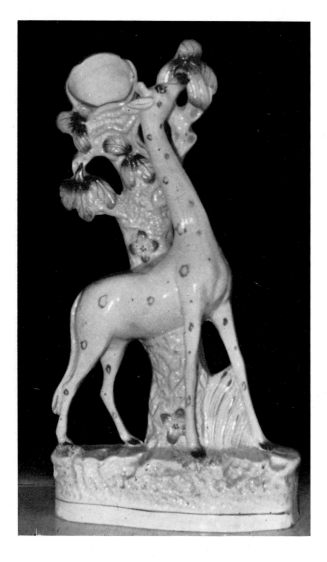

32. Robin, Edward Marshall Boehm, 1964 (p. 65)